JUST GOOD FOOD

HERE at last is a cookbook with a recipe for coq au vin that you won't need lessons from Le Cordon Bleu to follow, directions for making homemade fettucine and ravioli in four simple steps, and advice on how to make sinfully scrumptious desserts (raspberry and almond soufflé) that will stun your guests.

A firm believer that good food and arduous cooking don't have to be synonymous, Paul Rubinstein presents over 150 easy-to-follow recipes for appetizing, appealing dishes. From hors d'oeuvres such as avocado-tomato dip and mushrooms stuffed with chicken livers to soups, main courses, salads, and desserts, the recipes in this cookbook will surprise you with their elegant yet easy style, their unintimidating directions, and their delicious results.

Just Good Food is an eight-course banquet that new and experienced cooks alike will savor. The time-saving recipes run the gamut from basic, all-American favorites (such as turkey pot pie) to continental cuisine (Vichyssoise) to creative cookery (a broccoli soufflé). Preparing gourmet food needn't be restricted to culinary wizards, and Paul Rubinstein, author of and contributor to several other cookbooks, knows that everyone wants to eat just good food!

Also by Paul Rubinstein

Cookbooks

THE NIGHT BEFORE COOKBOOK
(co-author Leslie Rubinstein)

FEASTS FOR TWO

FEASTS FOR TWELVE (OR MORE)

Novel

THE PETRODOLLAR TAKEOVER
(co-author Peter Tanous)

JUST GOOD FOOD

Paul Rubinstein

CHARLES SCRIBNER'S SONS

NEW YORK

Copyright © 1978 Paul Rubinstein

Library of Congress Cataloging in Publication Data
Rubinstein, Paul.
  Just good food.

  Includes index.
    1. Cookery.   2. Cookery, International.   I. Title.
TX715.R9216   641.5   77-17408
ISBN 0-684-15526-5

1 3 5 7 9 11 13 15 17 19 Q/C 20 18 16 14 12 10 8 6 4 2

PRINTED IN THE UNITED STATES OF AMERICA

For Jason, my son

2003414

CONTENTS

INTRODUCTION

Probably the best way to describe what this book is, is to define clearly what it is not. It is not an attempt to create a new encyclopedia of cuisine. It is not an all-inclusive survey of the cooking techniques of a given country or of many countries. It is not a diet book, nor is it a budget book, nor does it contain a gimmick for shortcuts. It is not intended specifically for entertaining or for any particular season or event. It is not taken from the menus of great restaurants or hotels, and it has not been written with the advice of a White House chef or other such great personage.

Just Good Food offers popular food for Americans to serve at home, for guests or just family. Most of the ingredients are available year-round in one form or another (fresh, frozen, canned), and few are super-expensive. I hope this is a book you'll want to keep handy. Lists of ingredients and simple numbered instructions for each recipe can help you prepare a good meal, with about twenty choices for each course.

All the recipes are designed for six portions, and where an unusual piece of equipment might be needed I have said as much and described the item. All the recipes have been tested in my New York apartment kitchen, which is fairly standard except that it contains two refrigerators and two sinks. My range operates on natural gas and has two ovens.

I will not go into a long list of recommended pots and pans and other utensils here—there is plenty of literature on the subject, not excluding the housewares advertisements of the department stores. In the realm of measuring instruments, however, I strongly urge having an oven thermometer because the temperature setting of the oven control on a range can be off as much as 50 degrees. It also makes good sense to have an accurate timer or two with a good loud bell, and a balance scale (no springs!) for weighing roasts. The scale, by the way, is also handy if you suspect the printed weights on meat packages might be overstated by your friendly neighborhood supermarket. I also recommend a fat-candy thermometer and a big (4- to 6-cup) measure in the form of a pitcher as well as smaller ones.

Over the years I have often been asked whether I do "gourmet" cooking, or specialize in "gourmet" food, or other such questions. The word *gourmet* means a person who appreciates good food (and drink). It is meaningless as an adjective to me, as I cannot think of what the negative form would mean. Is a hot dog on a bun "non-gourmet"? Therefore, I say that "gourmet" food is *Just Good Food*.

PAUL RUBINSTEIN

I

Hors d'Oeuvres and Appetizers

AVOCADO-TOMATO DIP

A spicy dip to serve with cocktails, a cousin of guacamole.

3 large, just-ripe avocados
3 large tomatoes
1 small clove garlic
1 small onion
½ cup mayonnaise
½ teaspoon seasoned salt
¼ teaspoon freshly ground white pepper
8 drops Tabasco sauce *or* similar hot sauce

1. Pit and peel the avocados and place them in a blender jar.

2. Peel the tomatoes as follows. Spear each tomato with a long-handled fork and dip into boiling water for a few seconds until

the skin cracks in one or two places. Remove, allow to cool for just a few seconds, quarter, and peel. Skin should slip off easily. Remove the seeds from the quarters. Add peeled tomatoes to blender jar.

3. Peel and mince the garlic very fine and add to blender jar. Do the same with the onion. Add the mayonnaise, salt, pepper, and hot sauce. Run the blender for about 20 seconds or until the dip is well blended. If your blender is small you may want to divide up the ingredients and run them through in two shifts.

4. Serve with corn chips or potato chips. If you don't intend to serve the dip immediately, spread a thin layer of mayonnaise over the surface and refrigerate.

BAKED CLAMS OREGANATA

36 fresh medium- to large-size clams on the half shell
¼ pound butter
1 cup fine white bread crumbs
3 tablespoons oregano
1 small clove garlic, peeled and minced very fine
½ cup finely chopped parsley
¼ teaspoon freshly ground black pepper

1. Arrange the clams on the half shell in a baking pan or dish. Preheat oven to 425 degrees.

2. Melt the butter in a saucepan, taking care not to burn it or allow it to color. Remove from heat and stir in the bread crumbs, oregano, garlic, parsley, and pepper. Stir to blend thoroughly.

3. Spoon the bread-crumb mixture over the clams, dividing it equally among them.

4. Bake in the preheated oven 5 minutes and serve hot, six clams per portion.

COQUILLES ST. JACQUES

This dish of delicate scallops au gratin is often served in special shells, but ordinary ramekins may be used with equal success.

2 tablespoons chopped shallots
4 tablespoons butter
1 tablespoon olive oil
1 cup fresh finely chopped mushrooms
¼ teaspoon salt
⅛ teaspoon freshly ground white pepper
⅛ teaspoon nutmeg
½ cup dry white wine
1½ pounds fresh scallops
2 cups dry white bread crumbs
2 cups butter, melted
1 tablespoon lemon juice
1 tablespoon fresh chopped parsley

1. Sauté the shallots in 2 tablespoons of the butter and the oil for about 3 minutes until soft, then add the chopped mushrooms, salt, pepper, and nutmeg and cook gently over low heat for 10 minutes, stirring occasionally. Remove from heat and set aside.

2. Melt the other 2 tablespoons butter in a saucepan, add the white wine, and bring to a simmer. Add the scallops and simmer 6 minutes.

3. Arrange the moist mushroom mixture in the bottoms of six ramekins or shells, then place a portion of cooked scallops over the mushrooms and sprinkle on any cooking liquid left in the saucepan.

4. Cover the scallops with the bread crumbs and douse liberally with the melted butter, being careful to moisten all the surface of the bread crumbs.

5. Cook under broiler at medium-high heat as far away from the heating element as your broiler allows for about 10 minutes or until the surface is nicely browned but not burned.

6. Remove ramekins from broiler, sprinkle over each a little lemon juice and a pinch of parsley, and serve immediately.

CRAB MEAT SHELLS

2 tablespoons butter
1 pound cooked crab meat
6 slices bacon
½ teaspoon mustard powder
½ teaspoon seasoned salt
½ cup chili sauce
½ cup mayonnaise
1 tablespoon Maggi liquid seasoning *or* soy sauce
2 teaspoons lemon juice

1. Butter six shells or ramekins. Preheat oven to 325 degrees.

2. Divide the crab meat into six equal portions, place it in the buttered shells, and warm in the preheated oven 8 to 10 minutes.

3. Meanwhile, fry the bacon in a skillet, drain it on paper towels, and combine the mustard, salt, chili sauce, mayonnaise, Maggi, and lemon juice into a fairly thick sauce.

4. Turn on oven broiler to medium high. Spread the sauce over the crab meat in the shells, cook under broiler about 4 minutes, top each portion with a bacon strip, and serve hot.

CHEESE FONDUE

This festive dish is very easy to prepare, may be used not only as an hors d'oeuvre but also as a late-supper dish, and best of all is a marvelous way to use up those leftover pieces of slightly hardened cheese you would otherwise have thrown away. Although a fondue set complete with burner, copper pot, and long-handled forks is very attractive for serving, you can make do with a hot plate or warming tray, a nice clean saucepan from the kitchen, and regular forks.

2 pounds Swiss cheese (imported from Switzerland is best)
1 pound medium-sharp cheddar cheese
4 cups dry white wine
1 tablespoon arrowroot
1 teaspoon seasoned salt
1 teaspoon nutmeg
¼ teaspoon cayenne pepper (optional)
1 tablespoon Worcestershire sauce
2 long thin loaves crusty French or Italian bread, cut into bite-size pieces

1. Shred or grate the cheese.

2. In the fondue pot or other saucepan, bring all but ¼ cup of the wine to just below the boiling point over medium heat. Reduce heat to medium low and add the grated cheese, about ½ cup at a time, stirring each time until cheese is melted before adding the next handful.

3. Dissolve the arrowroot in the remaining ¼ cup of wine and stir into the mixture, then add seasoned salt, nutmeg, optional cayenne, and Worcestershire sauce.

4. Place fondue pot over burner or hot plate and serve alongside platter of bread pieces, providing longest possible forks. Heat should be adjusted so that fondue remains hot without bubbling. Spear the bread pieces with a fork, then dip them into the fondue and eat. When the fondue is almost finished, turn off the hot plate or burner. The crust that forms at the bottom of the pot is delicious.

EGGS IN ASPIC WITH CRAB MEAT

This is an elegant, eye-pleasing first course that takes a little longer than most to prepare, but makes up for it by letting you do the work a day or more in advance of serving.

1 pound scraps of fish, fish bones, heads, etc. (order from fish
    market or fish department at supermarket)
2 stalks celery, chopped into 1-inch pieces
2 carrots, peeled and chopped into 1-inch pieces
1 large onion, peeled and quartered
4 sprigs fresh parsley
1 cup white wine
2 quarts water
2 egg whites
3 envelopes unflavored gelatin
6 eggs
1 pound cooked crab meat, picked over to remove cartilage
2 cups mayonnaise
1 tablespoon lemon juice
¼ teaspoon salt
¼ teaspoon freshly ground white pepper
4 tablespoons chili sauce
1 tablespoon Worcestershire sauce

1. In a large saucepan combine the fish scraps, celery, carrots,
onion, parsley, wine, and water and simmer for about 1 hour or
until the liquid is reduced by one-half.

2. Remove from heat, strain
stock through a sieve to remove the vegetables and
fish bones, retaining stock,
then through a double
thickness of cheesecloth
wrung out in cold water.
Bring the strained stock to a

simmer again in a clean saucepan, then turn off heat, stir in the egg whites, let stand for 1 hour until the egg whites have gathered all the impurities, then strain through cheesecloth again. The result should be a crystal-clear, tasty fish stock.

3. Dissolve the gelatin powder in ½ cup cold water, add softened gelatin to the stock, and bring it to a simmer again, stirring until the gelatin is completely dissolved with no floating lumps. Allow it to cool while doing step 4.

4. Either soft-boil the 6 eggs for 4 minutes, then very carefully peel them; or poach them, one at a time, in a shallow pan of very hot water with a little vinegar added until the whites are firm and the yolks still soft, trimming the poached eggs after removing them from the water with a slotted spoon. Soft-boiling is easier and produces a nicer appearance in the final dish.

5. Arrange six 1-cup-capacity custard cups on a tray that will fit into your refrigerator. Pour a little stock into each to the depth of ¼ inch, refrigerate, and allow to jell firm (about 15 to 30 minutes). Place one cooked egg in each cup, fill with enough stock to barely cover the egg, and return to the refrigerator until again jelled firm.

6. Cover each egg with crab meat to the top of the cup, fill to the top with the stock, and refrigerate again. The cups should now remain in the refrigerator for at least 1 hour, until just before serving.

7. Combine the mayonnaise, lemon juice, salt, pepper, chili sauce, and Worcestershire sauce in a mixing bowl, mix well, and refrigerate. Mayonnaise dressings keep fairly well, so you can do this step of the recipe in advance.

8. To serve, dip each cup in some hot water for a few seconds, pass a sharp knife around the inside of the cup quickly, and unmold onto an individual plate or serving platter. Serve with the mayonnaise sauce.

OPTIONAL: If after preparing the eggs in aspic through step 6 you have any substantial amount of stock left, pour it into a jelly-roll pan to the depth of about ¼ inch and refrigerate. When serving, score the felled stock with a knife into small squares or diamonds, remove from the pan with a spatula, and use the cubed aspic as a garnish on the platter or individual plates.

FRESH FRUIT COCKTAIL

2 oranges
1 grapefruit
2 apples
1 banana
1 cantaloupe *or* other melon in season
12 strawberries
1 small bunch seedless green grapes
1 tablespoon lemon juice
1 tablespoon sugar
2 tablespoons kirsch
6 rounded leaves iceberg lettuce
6 maraschino cherries

1. Peel and section the oranges and the grapefruit, removing seeds and skins.

2. Peel, quarter, core, and slice the apples. Peel and slice the banana. Halve, scoop the pits and pulp out, and ball the melon with a melon baller. Wash the strawberries and remove stems. Wash and separate the grapes.

3. Place all the prepared fruit in a bowl, sprinkle on lemon juice, sugar, and kirsch, and let stand in refrigerator for at least 1 hour, overnight if possible.

4. To serve, arrange one lettuce leaf in each of six stemmed cocktail glasses, add mixed fruit, and top with maraschino cherry.

FRESH MUSHROOMS STUFFED WITH CHOPPED CHICKEN LIVERS

24 medium-size fresh mushrooms (1 to 1½ inches in diameter)
1 pound fresh chicken livers
¼ pound butter, softened
1 cup finely chopped onion
2 hard-cooked eggs, chopped fine
½ teaspoon salt
¼ teaspoon freshly ground black pepper
½ teaspoon seasoned salt

1. Wipe the mushrooms clean with a clean, damp cloth, carefully remove the stems from the caps with a twisting motion, set aside the caps, and chop the stems fine.

2. Drop the chicken livers into 2 quarts boiling water and simmer 5 minutes. Remove from water and drain.

3. Using 2 tablespoons of the butter, sauté the chopped onions and mushroom stems in a skillet until onions are softened and transparent but not browned. Remove onions and mushrooms from pan with a slotted spoon.

4. In a blender jar combine the cooked chicken livers, remaining soft butter, cooked onions and mushrooms, chopped eggs,

salt, and pepper, and run blender for 30 seconds or more until mixture is well blended. Remove to a bowl and refrigerate to chill thoroughly.

5. To serve, spoon the chicken-liver mixture into the mushroom caps, piling high, then sprinkle a little seasoned salt over the top of each.

HOME MARINATED HERRING

12 herring fillets (about 6 inches long)
2 cups sour cream
½ cup red wine vinegar
1 tablespoon fine olive oil
2 cups paper-thin onion slices
1 cup white radishes, peeled and cut into julienne strips
2 tablespoons lemon juice

1. Wash the herring fillets in cold running water; drain on paper towels, turning once.

2. In a shallow glass baking dish combine the sour cream, vinegar, oil, onion, radishes, and lemon juice. Stir to mix well.

3. Arrange herring fillets in the marinade so that they are completely covered.

4. Refrigerate one full day or longer before serving, basting occasionally. The herring can be sliced but are delicious served whole with fresh rye bread and butter.

HOT ONION-CHEESE TOASTS

12 thin slices white bread, crusts trimmed
8 ounces cream cheese, at room temperature
½ cup finely minced onion
1 cup finely grated Swiss cheese
1 teaspoon paprika

1. Toast the bread slices to a light gold color and set aside.

2. In a mixing bowl combine the cream cheese, minced onion, and grated Swiss cheese with a spoon, then blend thoroughly with a hand-held electric mixer.

3. Spread the toasts with the cheese and onion mixture, and sprinkle a tiny pinch of paprika over each for color.

4. Arrange the toasts on a cookie sheet and place in oven broiler under medium flame about 3 inches away from heating element for about 2 minutes or until top of cheese is lightly browned. Serve piping hot as hors d'oeuvres or appetizer. For bite-size hors d'oeuvres, quarter the cheese toasts after toasting.

MARINATED MUSHROOMS AND ONIONS

½ pound fresh mushrooms
2 large onions
1 cup dry white wine
2 cups French olive oil
½ cup vinegar
1 cup water
1 clove garlic, peeled and sliced
1 small bunch fresh parsley
1 teaspoon whole black peppercorns
½ teaspoon salt
1 lemon, sliced very thin

1. Quarter or halve the mushrooms into bite-size pieces, but leave smallest mushrooms whole. Peel and slice the onions.

2. Combine all the remaining ingredients in a large saucepan and bring to a boil. Turn off heat and let stand about 1 hour.

3. Add the mushrooms to the liquid, bring to a simmer, and cook at a simmer, uncovered, for 15 minutes. Turn off heat and allow the mushrooms in the liquid to cool completely to room temperature. Remove the mushrooms with a slotted spoon and set aside.

4. Add the sliced onions to the same liquid and bring to a simmer again. Cook 15 minutes, turn off heat, and allow to cool as before. Then add the mushrooms to the onions in the liquid.

5. Let the marinated mushrooms and onions stand at room temperature in their liquid until time to serve. Do not refrigerate.

MOLDED SALMON MOUSSE
GARNISHED WITH CUCUMBERS

2½ pounds fresh salmon (one piece)
1 cup water
1 cup dry white wine
½ cup clam juice
1 small onion, peeled and sliced
1 carrot, peeled and chopped
2 stalks celery, cut in 1-inch pieces
1 bay leaf
⅛ teaspoon freshly ground white pepper
3 envelopes unflavored gelatin powder
1 medium cucumber
2 egg whites
1 tablespoon Worcestershire sauce
2 cups light cream

1. Chill an 8-cup ring mold in the refrigerator. Preheat oven to 350 degrees.

2. In a saucepan or pot combine the piece of salmon with the water, wine, clam juice, onion, carrot, celery, bay leaf, and pepper. Cover and place in preheated oven. Cook 30 minutes until salmon is just cooked through to the bone. Test with a fork before removing from oven and cook a little longer if necessary. Cooking time depends partly on the thickness of the piece of salmon.

3. When cooked, remove the piece of salmon from the pot and set aside to cool on a plate. Reserve the liquid in the pot. Strain the liquid through two thicknesses of cheesecloth wrung out in cold water. Then dissolve the gelatin in water, add to the liquid,

and bring to a simmer over medium heat. Remove broth from heat and refrigerate until it just begins to jell slightly.

4. Peel and slice the cucumber into paper-thin slices. Line the bottom of the chilled mold with about ¼-inch depth of the almost jelled broth. Then add the cucumber slices to the bottom of the mold in an overlapping pattern, letting them stand partly up the rounded sides of the mold. Refrigerate the lined mold while completing the mousse.

5. Remove skin and bones from the cooled piece of salmon, and run the meat through the finest blade of a meat grinder or food mill.

6. In the bowl of an electric mixer combine the ground salmon, egg whites, and Worcestershire sauce and start mixing. Add the light cream about 1 tablespoon at a time until all of it is incorporated. Finally add the remainder of the partially jelled broth to the mousse and mix well.

7. Pour the mousse into the lined mold and refrigerate until it jells firm, approximately 3 to 4 hours.

8. To serve, dip the mold in hot water for a few seconds, then reverse onto a serving platter. Blot up any liquid with a paper towel. The result should be a shimmering pink circle of salmon mousse topped with the pale green cucumber slices looking like scales.

SEAFOOD COCKTAIL
(LAMAZE SAUCE)

The secret of excellence in a seafood cocktail is the freshness of the ingredients. Avoid using frozen seafood unless absolutely necessary. You may substitute the ordinary tomato-base cocktail sauce, but I resist it as too overpowering of the taste of the seafood.

2 lemons
12 fresh large shrimp, peeled and deveined
1 1½-pound live Maine lobster
2 cups fresh cooked lump crab meat
2 cups mayonnaise
¼ cup chili sauce
½ teaspoon salt
¼ teaspoon freshly ground white pepper
1 tablespoon Worcestershire sauce
6 lettuce leaves
1 hard-cooked egg, peeled

1. Bring about 3 quarts of water to a boil in a large saucepan, add one sliced lemon to the water, and drop in the peeled shrimp. Boil 4 minutes, remove shrimp from water, and allow to cool.

2. Drop the live lobster into the boiling water and boil 25 minutes. Remove from water and allow it to cool. Cut open the tail shell with a pair of shears, slicing through the segmented bottom of the shell, and remove the tail meat in one piece. Slice the tail into ¼-inch-thick round slices and then, using a toothpick, push out the little segment of intestine from each slice. Crack the claws and remove the meat, taking out the flat piece of cartilage. Crack smaller claw segments and remove lumps of meat. Set cooked lobster meat aside with the shrimp and the crab-meat lumps which were purchased precooked.

3. In a large mixing bowl combine the mayonnaise, chili sauce, salt, pepper, and Worcestershire sauce and mix well. Cut the remaining lemon into six wedges.

4. Add the cooked seafood to the sauce and mix gently to avoid breaking up the crab meat too much. Make sure all the seafood is well coated with sauce.

5. Using six cocktail glasses, insert one lettuce leaf in each as a liner, fill with one-sixth of the seafood cocktail, taking care that each glass gets two shrimp and a fair portion of lobster and crab. Spoon any remaining sauce over each. Place the hard-boiled egg in a sieve and rub through with a wooden spoon into a small bowl. Sprinkle some sieved egg over each cocktail.

6. Refrigerate cocktails until ready to serve, and serve garnished with lemon wedges, providing a small fork for each.

NOTE: If the recommended seafood is not available or too expensive, you may substitute cooked scallops, cooked chunks of any white fish, crayfish tails, or other seafood.

STEAK TARTARE CANAPÉS

1 pound freshly ground best-quality lean sirloin *or* round steak
1 egg yolk
¼ cup very finely minced onion
1 tablespoon fresh chopped parsley
2 teaspoons Worcestershire sauce
1 tablespoon fine olive oil
3 drops Tabasco *or* other hot sauce
1 loaf sandwich bread *or* dark pumpernickel, thinly sliced
2 small cans rolled anchovy fillets

1. In a mixing bowl, using your hands, mix the ground beef, egg yolk, onion, parsley, Worcestershire sauce, olive oil, and Tabasco.

2. Trim the crusts from the bread slices, spread with the beef mixture, and garnish each slice with an anchovy fillet.

3. Arrange canapés on a serving platter and chill until shortly before serving time.

STUFFED BRIOCHES

For those who may not know, a brioche is a soft French roll, shaped like a cupcake with a bump on top, made of a delicious golden-yellow dough. Brioches may be found at a good bakery.

12 small brioches
½ pound liverwurst
½ cup chopped boiled ham
¾ cup heavy cream
½ cup grated Parmesan cheese
2 tablespoons dry white wine
½ teaspoon salt
¼ teaspoon freshly ground black pepper

1. Preheat oven to 350 degrees.

2. Slice off the tops of the brioches and reserve them.

3. With your fingers pull out most of the soft dough from the brioches, leaving them as shells. Place bits of dough in a mixing bowl.

4. Remove skin and cut up the liverwurst into small dice. Add to the bowl, along with the ham, cream, cheese, wine, salt, and pepper.

5. Mix, then transfer the contents of the bowl to a heavy enameled saucepan. Cook over very low flame, stirring, until a thick paste is formed.

6. Spoon the hot filling into the brioche shells, replace tops, arrange on a cookie sheet, and bake 5 minutes in the preheated oven. Serve hot as appetizers or hors d'oeuvres.

NOTE: This savory appetizer goes particularly well with an aperitif wine. Also, if brioches are not available, you may use another kind of soft roll of similar shape.

STUFFED ENDIVES

6 heads Belgian endive
8 ounces cream cheese, at room temperature
3 tablespoons butter, softened
2 tablespoons blue cheese
1 tablespoon finely chopped chives
1 teaspoon seasoned salt

1. Wash and carefully separate the delicate leaves of the endive heads. Pat dry.

2. Cream together in a mixing bowl the cream cheese, butter, and blue cheese until well blended. Add the chives to the mixture and stir only enough to distribute them evenly.

3. Put the cheese filling into a pastry bag or tube with a decorative nozzle. Pipe the filling into the endive leaves, then sprinkle each with a small pinch of seasoned salt.

4. Arrange stuffed endives on a serving platter and keep chilled in refrigerator until serving time.

STUFFED GRAPE LEAVES

This is a Middle Eastern dish that is perfect for either a first course or an hors d'oeuvre. Although it may take more time, if you want to use it as an hors d'oeuvre I suggest making smaller, more numerous pieces than you would if they were being served at the table as a first course.

¼ cup olive oil
¾ cup chopped onion
1 pound ground lean beef *or* lamb
1 clove garlic, peeled and crushed through a press
¼ cup minced fresh parsley
¼ cup minced watercress
¼ teaspoon salt
1½ cups cooked rice
1 jar grape leaves packed in salt water (¾ pound to 1 pound net weight)
6 to 8 lamb *or* beef rib bones
1 pint sour cream or plain yogurt, chilled

1. Heat the oil in a skillet, add the onions, and cook gently over medium heat for about 4 minutes.

2. Add the meat, garlic, parsley, watercress, salt, and rice to the pan. Toss and cook just until meat browns slightly. Turn off heat and set skillet aside.

3. Open jar of leaves; lay them out one at a time on a board. Cut away any thick central stems left on as you go along. Place 1 to 2 tablespoons of the meat and rice mixture on each leaf, and roll up, tucking in the ends. For small hors d'oeuvres, cut leaves in half lengthwise and make smaller units.

4. In a fairly deep saucepan arrange the bones on the bottom as a fairly level layer. Add rolled grape leaves in layers, packed tightly. Pour 1½ cups of boiling water over the top, then place on top a heavy plate or saucepan cover one size smaller than the pan to weigh down the grape leaves.

5. Bring water to a simmer over medium heat and cook ½ hour. Add a little water if necessary during cooking. When done, allow to cool to room temperature, then refrigerate. Serve cold with sour cream or plain yogurt for a sauce.

STUFFED SALAMI AND PROSCIUTTO WITH MELON BALLS

This is an easy-to-make, elegant first course with a delicious combination of salty and sweet tastes.

2 8-ounce packages cream cheese, at room temperature
4 tablespoons sour cream
2 tablespoons fresh chopped dill
2 teaspoons lemon juice
1 teaspoon seasoned salt
18 paper-thin slices Genoa salami
18 paper-thin slices Italian prosciutto *or* German Westphalian ham
3 just-ripe cantaloupes

1. Cream together the cheese, sour cream, dill, lemon juice, and salt in a mixing bowl, using an electric mixer to make a smooth filling.

2. Place about 1 tablespoon of filling on each slice of salami and prosciutto, and roll up. If the meats are thin enough they should not require toothpicks to secure, but use them if needed.

3. Ball the cantaloupes with a mellon baller.

4. For each portion arrange a mound of melon balls in the center of a plate and surround with three each of the rolled salami and prosciutto. Chill until serving time.

TOASTED CHEESE ROLLS

12 tablespoons (1½ sticks) butter, softened
½ cup grated sharp cheddar cheese
¼ cup grated Swiss cheese
1 teaspoon Worcestershire sauce
1 teaspoon Dijon mustard
1 teaspoon paprika
1 loaf white bread, thinly sliced

1. Preheat oven broiler.

2. In a mixing bowl combine the butter, cheeses, Worcestershire sauce, mustard, and paprika.

3. Trim crusts from the bread slices.

4. Spread the bread slices with the cheese mixture as evenly as possible.

5. Roll them up and secure with toothpicks. Do not use plastic toothpicks as they may melt.

6. Arrange the cheese rolls on a cookie sheet and toast under the broiler until golden brown, when the cheese has melted slightly. Turn to toast second side. Serve hot.

TOMATOES STUFFED WITH TUNA SALAD

6 large, just-ripe tomatoes
1 8-ounce can best-quality white-meat tuna
1 cup mayonnaise
½ cup finely minced celery
1 tablespoon finely minced onion
½ teaspoon soy sauce
1 teaspoon mild mustard
¼ teaspoon salt
⅛ teaspoon freshly ground black pepper

1. Using a small, very sharp knife, carefully cut a round cap, 1½ inches in diameter, from the top of each tomato. Reserve caps. Remove as much pulp and seeds from the tomatoes as possible without damaging outer shape, using a small spoon or a melon baller.

2. Drain liquid from the tuna and place it in a mixing bowl. Break up the meat with a fork into small chunks, then add the mayonnaise, celery, onion, soy sauce, mustard, salt, and pepper. Mix well.

3. Stuff the tomatoes with the tuna mixture, piling it above the level of the top edges of the tomatoes. Top with the reserved tomato caps. Serve chilled.

II

Soups

ASPARAGUS TIP SOUP

1 large bunch fresh asparagus (about 1½ pounds)
8 cups chicken broth *or* chicken consommé
½ cup finely chopped onion
¼ cup minced celery
4 tablespoons butter
3 tablespoons flour
1 cup milk
½ teaspoon salt
¼ teaspoon freshly ground white pepper

1. Wash and tie the bunch of asparagus in two places with string. Steam the asparagus in a pot tall enough to cover after standing the bunch in it, thick ends down, in about 2 inches of water; boil for 15 minutes.

2. Remove the asparagus from the pot, remove the string, and cut off the tips, setting them aside.

3. In a saucepan combine the remaining thicker ends, the chicken broth, onion, and celery and simmer for about 15 minutes until the asparagus ends are very tender. Then force the mixture through a coarse sieve or run through a blender until smooth.

4. In a large double boiler, melt the butter, add the flour, and stir well, cooking the paste for 2 or 3 minutes. Add the milk, a little at a time, until it is incorporated, then add the soup mixture and seasonings. Stir and heat through in the double boiler over simmering water, adding the reserved asparagus tips for about 1 minute or just long enough to warm up before serving.

5. When serving make sure each person gets several tips.

BEEF BARLEY SOUP

1 1-ounce package dried mushrooms
6 cups beef broth *or* beef consommé
1 cup lean leftover cooked beef (brisket, steak, roast beef, etc.),
  cut into julienne strips
1½ cups cooked barley
½ teaspoon salt
¼ teaspoon freshly ground black pepper
1 teaspoon Maggi liquid seasoning (optional)

1. Add the dried mushrooms to the broth in a saucepan and bring to a boil. Reduce heat and simmer gently, covered, for 15 minutes.

2. Add the meat and cook 10 minutes longer, then add the cooked barley and cook 5 minutes more.

3. Season with salt, pepper, and the optional Maggi, and serve hot.

BEET SOUP

This recipe is for cold beet soup, an excellent summer méal-opener. To make it hot, follow the same directions, but add the sour cream after heating the soup and do not boil.

2 cups cooked beets (canned) with their liquid
½ cup sliced onion
2 tablespoons lemon juice
1 cup cooked mashed potatoes
1½ cups chicken broth *or* chicken consommé
1 cup sour cream
1 teaspoon salt

1. Puree the beets with the onion in a blender.

2. Combine the beet/onion puree with the remaining ingredients in a mixing bowl and beat at high speed with an electric mixer.

3. Chill; serve cold. If the soup stays a long time in the refrigerator it is a good idea to beat it again a minute or two before serving to prevent any separation of the various ingredients.

CAULIFLOWER SOUP

1 small or ½ large cauliflower head, trimmed
4 tablespoons butter
1 small or ½ large onion, peeled and thinly sliced
½ cup finely chopped celery
2½ cups chicken broth *or* chicken consommé
1 cup heavy cream
1 teaspoon salt
¼ teaspoon freshly ground white pepper
1 teaspoon Maggi liquid seasoning

1. On a steamer platform over boiling water in a deep saucepan equipped with a cover, steam the head of cauliflower for 30 to 45 minutes (depending on size) until tender. A knife should slide into the center with only a little pressure. Cool the cauliflower, then put it through a food mill using the fine blade to make a puree.

2. Melt the butter in a large saucepan and cook the onion and celery in it over medium heat until soft but not browned.

3. Add cauliflower puree and chicken broth. Bring to a boil, reduce heat, add cream, and heat again without allowing the soup to boil. Stir in salt, pepper, and Maggi seasoning and serve hot.

CHEDDAR CHEESE SOUP

This is a hearty, filling soup for a cold-weather meal.

¾ cup minced onion
¼ pound butter
8 tablespoons all-purpose flour
4 cups beef broth *or* beef consommé
1 cup grated sharp cheddar cheese, packed tightly
3 cups whole milk
2 tablespoons Worcestershire sauce
1 teaspoon seasoned salt
½ teaspoon freshly ground black pepper
½ cup finely minced parsley

1. In a large saucepan simmer the onions in the butter over medium heat until they are soft and transparent.

2. Stir in the flour to make a smooth paste and continue to cook 2 to 3 minutes.

3. Add the beef broth a little at a time, stirring to incorporate it and allowing the soup to thicken.

4. Add the cheese and stir until all is melted. Then add the milk, Worcestershire sauce, salt, and pepper. Heat the soup until it begins to simmer at the edges but do not boil. Keep hot until serving time and sprinkle some parsley over each serving as garnish.

CHICKEN BROTH WITH EGG DUMPLINGS

The best-tasting chicken broth, naturally, is one made from scratch. If you are not up to it, however, you may use any of the excellent canned broths or consommés available in the markets.

1 mature chicken (about 6 pounds)
4 carrots, peeled and chopped
1 turnip, peeled and cut into several pieces
2 stalks celery, cut into 1-inch pieces
4 large leeks, washed thoroughly and sliced fairly thin
2 onions, peeled and quartered
3 tablespoons butter
3 eggs
½ cup all-purpose flour
¼ teaspoon salt

1. Preheat oven to 450 degrees. Truss the chicken by tying the legs together and securing the wings close to the body with white string, and brown it in the oven for about 30 minutes, only long enough to turn the skin golden brown.

2. In a large, deep stockpot place the browned chicken, carrots, turnip, celery, leeks, and onions. Cover with 6 quarts of cold water, or more if necessary to cover the chicken by about 2 inches. Bring to a simmer, and cook gently for 4 or 5 hours. During this process you should skim the fat and scum from the surface frequently, occasionally wiping any accumulation from the inside of the pot just above the level of the liquid with a damp cloth.

3. When the broth is ready, having acquired a rich taste from the ingredients, strain it, removing the carcass of the chicken and the vegetables. Let it stand for 30 minutes and skim a final time, removing any remaining fat and scum. Place the broth in a clean saucepan and bring to a simmer while you prepare the dumpling batter.

4. Soften the butter by working it in a mixing bowl with a wooden spoon, beat in the eggs, then stir in the flour and the salt. Mix well until a smooth batter is formed. Using a standard teaspoon, drop spoonfuls of batter into the simmering broth and cook, covered, for 10 minutes, making sure the broth does not boil heavily. Serve hot.

NOTE: It is not a good idea to cook the dumplings in the soup far in advance of serving and then reheat it later, because the dumplings will tend to fall apart. You may prepare the batter ahead and refrigerate it, but the actual cooking should be done only a few minutes before the start of the meal.

COLD AVOCADO SOUP

4 just-ripe avocados
1 large cucumber
2 cups chicken broth *or* chicken consommé
2 cups half and half (½ cream, ½ milk)
2 teaspoons seasoned salt
¼ teaspoon freshly ground white pepper
3 teaspoons lemon juice
1 tablespoon chopped parsley
1 cup peeled, seeded, and diced fresh tomato

1. Peel, pit, and cut the avocados into chunks. Peel, seed, and slice the cucumber. Assemble in a bowl with the chicken broth, half and half, salt, pepper, and lemon juice.

2. Ladle some of the mixture into a blender jar and blend until pureed. Continue until all has been blended.

3. Chill the soup well.

4. To serve, ladle a portion of soup into each plate; garnish with a pinch of chopped parsley and 2 tablespoons of diced tomato.

COLD CUCUMBER SOUP

This is ideal for a light summer lunch, served with hot garlic bread or a toasted sandwich.

1 clove garlic, peeled and crushed through a press
3 tablespoons fine olive oil
2 large cucumbers, peeled and chopped
3 cups sour cream
1 tablespoon lemon juice
1 teaspoon Worcestershire sauce
½ teaspoon salt
¼ teaspoon freshly ground white pepper
1 tablespoon fresh chopped dill

1. Make sure the major ingredients are well chilled before starting, and use a mixing bowl that has been chilled in the freezer for about 1 hour.

2. Combine all the ingredients in the bowl and beat well with an electric mixer until blended. Chill well.

2003414

CORN CHOWDER

8 slices bacon, cut into 1-inch pieces
1 medium or 2 small onions, peeled and thinly sliced
4 tablespoons butter
3 tablespoons yellow cornmeal
2 cups chicken broth
½ teaspoon salt
¼ teaspoon freshly ground white pepper
2 cups canned or frozen cooked corn kernels, *or* fresh uncooked
    corn kernels stripped from the ears
2 cups heavy cream

1. Sauté the bacon pieces lightly with the onion slices over medium to low heat just long enough to soften the onions. Remove from heat and pour off bacon fat. Drain bacon and onion slices on paper towels.

2. In a large saucepan melt the butter and stir into it the cornmeal to make a smooth paste. Add the chicken broth, a little at a time, stirring to incorporate it.

3. Add the salt and pepper, corn kernels, drained bacon, and onions, and bring the soup to a simmer, stirring occasionally. Simmer 5 minutes.

4. Reduce heat, stir in the cream, and heat again without allowing the soup to boil. Serve hot.

CREAM OF CHICKEN SOUP

6 cups chicken broth *or* chicken consommé
4 tablespoons butter
4 tablespoons flour
1 cup cubed cooked chicken meat
1 cup heavy cream
1 tablespoon fresh chopped parsley
½ teaspoon salt
¼ teaspoon freshly ground white pepper

1. Heat the chicken broth in a saucepan, but do not allow it to boil.

2. In a second saucepan, melt the butter, add the flour, and stir into a paste. Cook over medium heat for 2 minutes, then add the hot broth, a little at a time, cooking and stirring until all the broth has been incorporated and the soup has thickened.

3 Add the cubed chicken meat and heat 5 more minutes, then reduce heat and add the cream, parsley, salt, and pepper. Bring to a simmer again without allowing the soup to boil. Serve immediately or keep hot on a warming tray until service.

OPTIONAL: Cooked rice or cooked noodles may be added to the soup.

CREAM OF MUSHROOM SOUP

1 1-ounce package dried mushrooms (European variety if possible)
2 cups boiling water
1 dozen medium-size fresh mushrooms (about ½ pound, depending on size)
6 tablespoons butter
½ teaspoon salt
¼ teaspoon freshly ground black pepper
1 teaspoon Worcestershire sauce
2 tablespoons flour
2 cups beef broth *or* beef consommé
2 cups light cream

1. Immerse the dried mushrooms in the boiling water (off heat) and let them soak 15 minutes until the water turns the color of

strong tea. If the dried mushrooms are very light colored the water will be correspondingly lighter.

2. While the dried mushrooms soak, wash, then separate the fresh mushroom caps from the stems with a gentle twisting motion. Slice the caps into thin (⅛-inch) slices. Mince the stems.

3. Melt the butter in a 3-quart saucepan over medium heat. Add the sliced caps, salt, pepper, and Worcestershire sauce and simmer about 5 minutes over low heat until the mushrooms are soft. Remove them from the pan with a slotted spoon and drain on paper towels, leaving the butter and juices in the pan.

4. Remove the soaked dried mushrooms from their liquid, reserving the liquid. Mince them, and add them to the saucepan along with the minced fresh stems. Sauté the minced mushrooms over medium heat for 3 minutes.

5. Add the flour to the pan and stir with the minced mushrooms, cooking over medium heat for 2 minutes.

6. Add the mushroom liquid, little by little, stirring and cooking until well blended with the flour paste. Add the beef broth and bring to a simmer. At this point you may remove from heat and stop, leaving the remaining steps until just before serving.

7. Add the sliced mushrooms and the light cream to the soup and heat to just under the boiling point. Do not allow the soup to boil after adding the cream. Serve.

OPTIONAL: For added body, in step 6 when the soup is simmering, break 2 eggs into the soup and immediately break with a fork or wire whisk until the eggs form "strings."

FISH CHOWDER

This recipe is intended as a soup, but by increasing the quantity it can become a main course.

3 pounds assorted pieces of white fish such as cod, haddock, flounder, pike, or bass
2 carrots, peeled and chopped
2 stalks celery, chopped
1 large onion, peeled and sliced
2 tablespoons white vinegar
1 pound fish scraps, including heads, tails, and bones
2 cups cubed boiled potatoes
1 cup heavy cream

1. In a large saucepan combine the 3 pounds of fish, carrots, celery, onion, and vinegar with 1 quart of water; bring to a simmer and cook, covered, for 20 minutes.

2. Remove from heat and remove the pieces of fish from the broth with a slotted spoon onto a board. Remove all bones and skin from cooked fish, cut the fish into generous bite-size pieces, and set them aside in a bowl.

3. Return the bones and scraps from the cooked fish plus the 1 pound of other scraps to the pot, add another quart of water, and cook at a simmer, covered, for 1 hour.

4. Strain the soup through a fine strainer. Add the potatoes and cream to the broth, then the cooked pieces of fish. Bring to a simmer without allowing it to boil, and serve hot. I suggest not adding any salt and pepper until the soup reaches the table.

LENTIL SOUP

2 cups dry lentils
8 slices hickory-smoked bacon
1 cup finely chopped onion
4 cups beef broth *or* beef consommé
½ cup Madeira wine
1 bay leaf
¼ cup heavy cream
½ cup diced cooked ham
½ teaspoon seasoned salt
¼ teaspoon freshly ground black pepper

1. Soak the lentils in cold water to cover for several hours or overnight.

2. In a deep saucepan cook the bacon slices with the onion over medium heat until the onions soften slightly. The bacon should not brown very much and definitely should not get crisp.

3. Drain the lentils in a colander or strainer; add them to the saucepan, together with the broth, wine, and bay leaf. Cover, bring to a simmer, and cook about 25 minutes until lentils are quite tender.

4. Remove the bay leaf and rub soup through a strainer to produce a medium-thick puree.

5. Return the puree to the saucepan and stir in heavy cream, diced ham, salt, and pepper. Heat again but do not allow the soup to boil. Serve hot.

MIXED VEGETABLE SOUP

3 tablespoons butter
½ cup chopped carrots
½ cup chopped onion
½ cup chopped celery
2 cups peeled, seeded, and chopped tomatoes
4 cups chicken broth *or* chicken consommé
½ cup peeled and cubed potatoes
2 tablespoons fresh chopped parsley
½ teaspoon seasoned salt
¼ teaspoon freshly ground black pepper

1. Melt the butter in a skillet and brown the carrots, onions, and celery in it, stirring frequently. Remove the vegetables with a slotted spoon and place them in a soup kettle.

2. Add the tomatoes, broth, potatoes, and parsley, bring to a simmer, and cook, covered, for 40 minutes, adjusting heat to avoid fast boiling.

3. Season with the salt and pepper and serve hot.

NAVY BEAN SOUP

1 pound dry navy beans
1 ham bone (from a smoked ham with some meat on it) *or* 1 ham
   hock
4 tablespoons butter
1 cup finely chopped onion
½ teaspoon seasoned salt
¼ teaspoon freshly ground black pepper

1. Wash the beans in a strainer under cold running water, discarding any discolored ones. Soak them overnight in cold water to cover.

2. Drain the soaked beans. Place them in a deep saucepan and pour over them 2 quarts of boiling water. Add ham bone to the pot, cover, and simmer 1½ hours.

3. Melt the butter in a small saucepan without browning over low heat. Add the chopped onions and cook gently until the onions are soft (about 5 minutes). Add them to the soup, removing them with a slotted spoon to leave behind as much of the butter as possible.

4. Take out the ham bone, cut off the meat, and cut it into thin strips. Discard the bone and return the meat to the soup.

5. Skim the fat from the surface of the soup, season the soup with salt and pepper, stir, and keep hot until serving time. If soup has thickened too much, stir in a little boiling water or boiling beef consommé to dilute.

NEW ENGLAND CLAM CHOWDER

If you can get fresh clams to make this soup, by all means do so, but the canned minced clams in the recipe will yield an excellent chowder, too.

3 dozen fresh clams *or* 3 cups canned minced clams (with their juice)
2 cups chopped onion
6 tablespoons butter
3 medium-size potatoes, peeled and cubed
2 cups milk
2 cups heavy cream
2 tablespoons chopped parsley

1. Steam the fresh clams until they open over 2 cups of boiling water. Remove the clams from their shells, discarding the shells and any clams that do not open. Set aside the meat and reserve the water from the steaming, adding to it enough water to make about 5 cups. If you are using canned clams, drain them and add enough water to their liquid to make 5 cups.

2. Brown the onions in the butter over medium heat until they are golden, then add the 5 cups of liquid and the potatoes and cook until the potatoes are tender but not too soft, about 15 minutes.

3. Add the milk, cream, parsley, and reserved clams and bring to a simmer before serving, but do not boil after the cream has been added. Since the clams are salty, do not salt until the soup reaches the table and has been tasted.

OYSTER OR CLAM STEW

4 tablespoons butter
1 tablespoon very finely minced onion
½ clove garlic, peeled and crushed through a press
1 teaspoon paprika
2 tablespoons Worcestershire sauce
1 pint oysters, cleaned and shucked, *or* clams, with their liquor
2 cups half and half (½ milk, ½ cream)
½ teaspoon seasoned salt
½ cup sherry

1. In the top of a double boiler over simmering water melt the butter, add the onion and garlic, and cook about 5 minutes until softened.

2. Add paprika and Worcestershire sauce, stir, and cook 2 more minutes.

3. Add the oysters or clams and their juice, the half and half, and the salt. Continue cooking until the stew is hot but not boiling. Stir occasionally to prevent formation of a skin.

4. Just before serving, add the sherry and stir 1 minute to blend.

5. Serve the stew hot, with crusty hot bread, or add a slice of toasted bread, buttered and sprinkled with a little paprika for color, to each serving.

SPLIT PEA SOUP WITH CROUTONS

2 cups split peas
1 ham bone
½ cup chopped carrots
1 cup finely chopped onion
1 bay leaf
¼ teaspoon salt
¼ teaspoon freshly ground black pepper
6 tablespoons butter
3 cups ½-inch cubes of white bread

1. Wash the split peas under cold running water, then soak (in a large saucepan) in 3 quarts of water for several hours. Add the ham bone to the peas, bring to a simmer, and cook 2 hours, covered.

2. Add the carrots, onions, bay leaf, salt, and pepper and cook for an additional 30 minutes, covered.

3. Remove the ham bone and strain the soup, rubbing the peas and other vegetables through with a wooden spoon. Return to heat and keep hot while preparing croutons.

4. Melt the butter in a large skillet (cast iron is best), add the bread cubes, and brown them on all sides, turning frequently to prevent burning. Drain them on paper towels for a minute or two before serving. Serve hot soup with croutons sprinkled on top.

TOMATO BISQUE WITH RICE

6 large ripe tomatoes
6 cups chicken broth *or* chicken consommé
4 tablespoons butter
4 tablespoons flour
1 6-ounce can tomato paste
¾ cup heavy cream
2 cups cooked rice
½ teaspoon salt
¼ teaspoon freshly ground white pepper

1. Peel the tomatoes (see page 2), cut them into quarters, and carefully remove all the seeds from the centers. Place them in a large saucepan with the chicken broth and simmer gently, covered, for about 40 minutes, or until the tomato quarters begin to fall apart.

2. Melt the butter in another saucepan, add the flour, stir into a paste, and cook for 2 minutes without allowing the paste to brown. Add the tomato paste and blend well, then add the tomato-chicken broth, a little at a time, stirring and cooking to blend well.

3. Add the cream, the rice, and the seasonings to the soup and bring it to a simmer without letting it boil. Serve hot.

VICHYSSOISE (*Hot or Cold*)

6 medium-size leeks
4 medium-size potatoes
2 tablespoons butter
2 cups chicken broth *or* chicken consommé
½ teaspoon salt
2 cups milk
1 cup heavy cream
2 tablespoons fresh chopped chives
   black pepper freshly ground in a pepper mill

1. Wash the leeks thoroughly in cold water, cut away the green ends, and finely mince the white parts. Peel and slice the potatoes into ⅛-inch slices.

2. Melt the butter over medium-low heat in a large saucepan, add the minced leeks, and cook slowly for 15 minutes. Do not allow the leeks to color.

3. Add the sliced potatoes, chicken broth, and salt and simmer for another 15 minutes over low heat. When almost done, boil the milk in a separate saucepan, turn off heat under the soup, and add the milk to it. Now strain the mixture into another container, rubbing the leeks and potatoes through.

4. If you plan to serve cold Vichyssoise, stir in the heavy cream and refrigerate until well chilled. To serve, sprinkle chopped chives and fresh pepper from the mill over each serving.

5. To serve the soup hot, add cream and heat over a low flame until hot but not boiling. Do not allow the soup to boil after adding the cream. Sprinkle chives and pepper on top and serve.

III

Eggs and Pastas

EGGS BENEDICT

I recommend portions of one egg per person when serving this classic dish. Not only is it very rich and filling, but poaching twelve eggs and still serving them warm is rather tricky for the average-size kitchen. And considering the content of the Hollandaise sauce, each portion contains more than one egg anyway!

3 English muffins
6 slices cooked ham
1 tablespoon butter
6 eggs
12 tablespoons (1½ sticks) butter
4 egg yolks
2 teaspoons lemon juice
¼ teaspoon salt
1 teaspoon paprika

1. Split and toast the muffins, then arrange them cut side up on a platter and keep warm in the oven at low temperature. Trim the ham slices to just overlap the muffins and place one slice on each muffin.

2. Butter the cups of a six-section egg poacher, using 1 tablespoon butter, and bring about 1½ inches of water to a boil in the lower section. Break an egg into each cup, cover the poacher, and allow the eggs to cook over simmering water for about 5 to 6 minutes until the whites are cooked and the yolks still soft.

3. While the eggs are poaching, divide the butter into three equal parts of 4 tablespoons (½ stick) each. In a double boiler over simmering water, using a wire whisk, beat the egg yolks and lemon juice with one-third of the butter until the butter is

melted; add the next third and continue beating until it melts; then add the final piece and continue heating until the sauce thickens. Off heat, stir in the salt.

4. Step 3 should be timed so that the poached eggs are ready just about when the sauce is completed. Bring out the platter, and reverse each poached egg cup over one of the muffins to transfer the egg onto the ham slice. Spoon over each a generous spoonful of Hollandaise so as to cover the egg completely, sprinkle a little paprika over the eggs for decoration, and serve immediately while hot.

TOMATO-DEVILED EGGS

12 eggs
½ cup thick tomato paste (canned)
¼ cup mayonnaise
1 teaspoon curry powder
½ teaspoon salt
1 teaspoon lemon juice

1. Place the eggs in cold water to cover in a deep saucepan. Bring to a boil, turn off heat, and let stand, covered, for 20 minutes.

2. Run cold water over the eggs. Peel them, cut them in half, remove hard-cooked yolks, and refrigerate the egg white halves.

3. Rub two of the yolks through a sieve into a small cup and reserve.

4. Mash remaining yolks in a bowl and combine with the tomato paste, mayonnaise, curry powder, salt, and lemon juice. Mix well until smooth.

5. Using a pastry bag or tube (this cuts down on mess), pipe the filling through a decorative nozzle into the chilled egg white cavities, piling it above the level of the cut.

6. Sprinkle each deviled egg with a pinch of the sieved yolks and chill until time to serve.

DEEP-FRIED EGGS ON TOAST

A new way to make eggs, sure to intrigue, producing a different texture, but hot and delicious. I suggest doing only two eggs at a time and serving one person at a time.

6 large pieces of toast
1 quart or more vegetable oil for frying
12 eggs
1 tablespoon salt
1 teaspoon freshly ground black pepper

1. Arrange warm toast on six plates.

2. Heat the oil in a small but deep saucepan until it sizzles loudly and spatters when you drop in a drop of water. Do not allow the oil to smoke.

3. Break one egg into each of two custard cups. Add a pinch of salt and a smaller pinch of pepper to each. Slide the eggs, one right after the other, into the hot oil. Immediately insert a large cooking spoon (or two—one in each hand) and cup the whites around the yolks to hold them together for a few seconds until they solidify.

4. Cook 1 minute. Remove eggs onto toast with a slotted spoon. Repeat the process for each portion of two eggs.

POACHED EGGS WITH MUSHROOM SAUCE

4 ounces dried mushrooms (European if possible)
12 medium-size fresh mushrooms
8 tablespoons (1 stick) butter
4 tablespoons flour
3 cups beef broth *or* beef consommé
¼ teaspoon seasoned salt
⅛ teaspoon freshly ground black pepper
4 tablespoons butter
12 eggs
6 pieces white bread, toasted (optional)

1. Put the dried mushrooms into a small bowl and cover them with boiling water. Let stand at least 1 hour until the water turns dark brown and the mushrooms are soft.

2. Wash, then slice the fresh mushrooms into ⅛-inch slices. Sauté the slices in 4 tablespoons of the butter, tossing them frequently, until they soften. Turn off heat and set aside.

3. In a double boiler over simmering water, melt the other 4 tablespoons butter, add the flour, and stir into a paste, cooking for at least 2 minutes. Add the beef broth, a little at a time, stirring constantly, incorporating the liquid into the sauce, then do the same with the liquid from the European mushrooms. Chop the European mushrooms fine and add them to the sauce, followed

by the sliced mushrooms and their liquid from the pan. Add salt and pepper, and keep the sauce hot while preparing the eggs.

4. Poach the eggs in two six-egg poaching pans, having buttered the individual egg cups first. Cook over simmering water until the whites are firm and the yolks still soft.

5. Transfer the poached eggs very carefully onto warmed serving plates or onto toast. Ladle the hot mushroom sauce generously over the poached eggs and serve immediately.

HOT SCRAMBLED EGG RING WITH BACON BITS

This is a handy solution to serving breakfast to guests without having to prepare eggs separately for each person.

12 slices lean bacon
18 eggs
1 cup whole milk *or* half and half (½ milk, ½ cream)
½ teaspoon salt
9 tablespoons butter

1. Fry the bacon until crisp, drain on paper towels, crumble the bacon, and place it in a bowl handy to the stove.

2. Break the eggs into a bowl, add the milk and salt, and beat to blend well.

3. With 1 tablespoon of the butter, butter the inside of an 8-cup ring mold and place handy to the stove. Preheat oven to 400 degrees.

4. Melt the remaining butter (8 tablespoons) in a large skillet

over medium heat. When the butter is about half melted, pour in the eggs and stir quickly, scrambling the eggs, not allowing them to burn on the bottom. When the eggs have solidified only slightly but remain runny, quickly remove from heat and pour half the eggs into the mold. Spread them around in a level layer, then make a layer of the crumbled bacon bits. Top with the other half of the eggs.

5. Place the mold in the preheated oven and bake about 5 minutes until the eggs are firm. You can test by slipping a small knife into the eggs and moving it to one side, observing whether the eggs are set in the center or still too runny.

6. Unmold the ring onto a warm platter by placing the platter upside down over the mold, grasping both with both hands (using potholders) and quickly reversing. Serve hot.

SHIRRED EGGS WITH HAM

I don't particularly like fried ham, but I love the combination of ham and eggs. This recipe is a solution to that problem, with the added attractions of neat and easy service and a guarantee that the eggs stay hot.

3 tablespoons butter
6 slices cooked ham
2 tablespoons chopped chives
12 eggs
¾ cup heavy cream

1. Butter six 7-inch ovenproof ramekins generously and preheat the oven to 325 degrees.

2. In each ramekin place one slice of ham, sprinkle it with the chives, open two eggs carefully into each without breaking the yolks, and add 2 tablespoons of cream to each ramekin.

3. Bake in the preheated oven for 25 minutes, remove, and serve immediately. This baking time should yield firm whites and still-soft yolks, but it is a good idea to check after about 20 minutes by jiggling a ramekin slightly to make sure the yolks have not hardened. Salt and pepper should be provided at the table.

WESTERN SCRAMBLED EGGS

8 eggs
¼ cup cream
½ teaspoon salt
¼ teaspoon freshly ground black pepper
¼ cup fresh chopped chives
6 tablespoons butter
1½ cups cooked corn kernels, drained
½ cup chopped green pepper
1 tablespoon chopped pimientos

1. Beat the eggs with the cream, salt, pepper, and chives in a bowl.

2. In a wide skillet melt the butter, add the corn, peppers, and pimientos, and stir over medium heat for about 8 minutes.

3. Add the beaten eggs, mix with the corn and peppers, and cook 3 or 4 minutes until eggs are set but not hardened. Serve hot immediately.

PLAIN OMELETTE AND VARIOUS FILLINGS

Although the recipes in this book are intended for six people, the omelette must be an exception. Omelettes must be prepared one at a time, and served and consumed immediately. They should not be kept warm while others are being made. If you must prepare omelettes for several people at one meal, it is very important to measure and arrange the ingredients for all before beginning. Then the technique below can be followed to produce an omelette every 2 or 3 minutes, an acceptable time to serve six people. This recipe is for one three-egg omelette. For more you may multiply the ingredients by the number of people to be served.

PLAIN OMELETTE

3 eggs
1 pinch of salt
1 tablespoon butter

1. Warm a dinner plate in a 200-degree oven.

2. Heat an omelette pan or skillet (about 9 or 10 inches in diameter with curved rather than perpendicular sides) over medium flame until a drop of water released on the surface bounces.

3. While pan is heating, beat the eggs with the salt and 1 teaspoon cold water, just enough to blend the yolks and the whites. Have ready in a small bowl.

4. When the pan is ready, drop in the butter, immediately pour in the egg mixture, and stir vigorously with a fork, meanwhile shaking the pan back and forth with the other hand.

5. When the top of the omelette has begun to set but is still quite moist, tilt the pan forward (away from you) and carefully turn omelette to fold approximately in half. The best implement for this is a long, thin, flexible-bladed spatula.

6. As soon as folding is complete, reverse omelette onto warm plate and serve immediately.

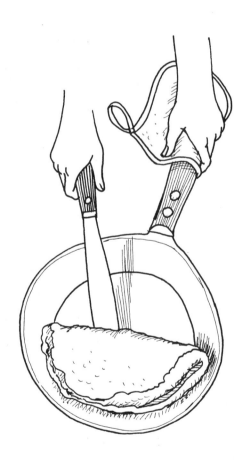

OMELETTE FILLINGS

A three-egg omelette will hold 3 to 4 tablespoons filling. This may be warm or at room temperature but should not be chilled. To make a filled omelette, simply spoon 3 or 4 tablespoons of prepared filling over the top of the omelette in step 5, just before folding. After the transfer to the serving plate, another spoonful of filling may be placed on top or alongside the finished omelette as a garnish (and to indicate to the consumer what to expect inside). The fillings below are sufficient to fill six omelettes.

CURRIED CRAB MEAT FILLING

1 tablespoon butter
2 tablespoons finely minced onion
1 tablespoon flour
2 teaspoons curry powder
1 cup clam juice
⅛ teaspoon freshly ground black pepper
1½ cups fresh cooked crab meat, picked over

1. Melt the butter in a small saucepan. Add the onion and cook for 2 or 3 minutes until softened.

2. Stir in flour and curry powder to make a paste. Cook 2 more minutes.

3. Add clam juice, a little at a time, stirring, until fairly thick sauce is achieved. Season with pepper.

4. Stir in crab meat, turn several times to coat it well. Keep warm over very low heat and spoon into omelette at appropriate time (step 5).

CURRIED SHRIMP, LOBSTER, SCALLOP, AND FISH FILLINGS

Substitute 1½ cups of sliced, cooked shrimp, cooked lobster meat, cooked small scallops, or chunked fish fillets for the crab meat in the preceding recipe.

CREAMED CHICKEN FILLING

1 tablespoon butter
1 tablespoon flour
2 teaspoons finely minced pimientos
1 cup chicken broth *or* chicken consommé
1½ cups diced cooked chicken

1. Melt the butter in a small saucepan, stir in the flour, and stir into a paste. Cook 2 or 3 minutes and add pimientos.

2. Add chicken broth a little at a time, stirring constantly, until a fairly thick sauce is achieved.

3. Add cooked chicken, turn over to coat meat with sauce, keep warm, and spoon into omelette at appropriate time (step 5).

CHICKEN LIVER FILLING

1½ cups fresh chicken livers
3 tablespoons butter
½ teaspoon salt
⅛ teaspoon freshly ground black pepper

1. Carefully cut the tendons out of the livers and cut each liver segment in half to make bite-size pieces.

2. Melt the butter in a small skillet, add livers, and brown them on all sides quickly, cooking a total of about 2 minutes. Sprinkle on salt and pepper.

3. Keep chicken livers warm and spoon into omelette at appropriate time (step 5).

JAM OR JELLY FILLING

Transfer jam or jelly from jar into a bowl and stir to loosen up. Spoon directly into omelette at step 5, but use only 2 tablespoons per omelette.

GREEN PEPPERS STUFFED WITH POACHED EGGS

6 tablespoons butter
1 cup finely minced onion
1 cup uncooked rice
2½ cups chicken broth *or* chicken consommé
½ cup grated Parmesan cheese
1 1-pound can stewed tomatoes
2 tablespoons flour
½ cup tomato paste
1 cup beef broth *or* beef consommé
6 fresh green peppers
6 eggs
2 tablespoons white vinegar

1. In a deep saucepan equipped with a cover, melt 4 table-spoons of the butter, add the onions, and cook slowly until the onions are softened, about 3 minutes. Then add the rice and the chicken broth and bring to a boil, stir once to unstick rice, reduce heat, and simmer, covered, until all liquid is absorbed (about 15 minutes). Move the pan of rice to a warming tray, add Parmesan, toss the rice with the cheese to mix well, cover, and keep hot.

2. While the rice is cooking you can begin the other prepara-tions. Run the stewed tomatoes through a blender. Melt the remaining 2 tablespoons of butter in a saucepan and stir in the flour to make a smooth paste; cook 3 minutes over medium heat. Stir in the blended tomatoes, the tomato paste, and the beef broth. Simmer sauce about 15 to 20 minutes until it is thick and smooth.

3. Cut the tops off the peppers, dig out the seeds and pulp, and blanch the shells in boiling water 1½ minutes, including the tops. Remove from water and arrange peppers on a warm serv-ing platter.

4. Bring 2 quarts of water to a boil in a large skillet. Break the eggs into custard cups. Add the vinegar to the boiling water. Turn off heat and slip the eggs into the water, disturbing them as little as possible. Let them poach in the hot water 6 to 8 min-utes until whites are firm but yolks still soft.

5. To assemble, fill peppers one-third full of hot rice. Slip one poached egg, removing it from water with a slotted spoon, into each pepper. Add more rice to fill, spoon some tomato sauce over the top, replace cap, and serve hot with additional sauce on the side.

EGG NOODLES WITH HAM AND MUSHROOM BITS

3 cups all-purpose flour
4 eggs
6 tablespoons butter
¼ pound fresh mushrooms, chopped fine
1 tablespoon Worcestershire sauce
¼ teaspoon seasoned salt
⅛ teaspoon freshly ground black pepper
¼ pound cooked ham, sliced and cut into ¼-inch squares

1. Combine the flour and eggs in a bowl. Stir until thoroughly mixed and then knead by hand until a mass is formed. Transfer to a lightly floured board and continue to knead until dough is quite stiff. You may use the dough hook of a kitchen processor if you have one.

2. Separate dough into at least two portions. Roll out each part to a thickness of about ⅛ inch and let it stand 1 hour. Cut into ½-inch-wide strips and either lay out on a counter or hang over a line until dry and brittle, about 1 to 2 hours.

3. To cook, bring 4 to 6 quarts of water to a boil in a large stockpot. While water is heating, melt the butter in a small skillet over medium heat. Add the chopped mushrooms, Worcestershire sauce, salt, and pepper and cook about 6 to 8 minutes. Turn off heat, cover skillet, and keep warm.

4. Drop the dry noodles into the boiling water a few at a time so that water continues to boil between additions. When all are in, time exactly 8 minutes.

5. Drain the noodles in a colander, return them to the pot, add warm mushrooms and the ham squares, toss to mix well, and serve hot. The heat from the noodles will be sufficient to warm up the ham squares, which should be at room temperature at time of adding.

FETTUCCINE ALFREDO

1 2-pound package egg noodles
1 egg yolk
1 cup heavy cream
4 tablespoons butter
½ teaspoon salt
1 cup freshly grated Parmesan cheese
½ teaspoon freshly ground black pepper

1. Prepare the noodles according to package directions, cooking 1 minute less than indicated. Drain in a colander and proceed with the following steps quickly while noodles are hot.

2. Beat the egg yolk into the cream, then put this mixture and the butter into a large, heavy saucepan big enough to hold all the noodles easily.

3. Cook over medium heat, stirring, for about 1 minute, then add the drained noodles, salt, and Parmesan. Toss the noodles well to coat with sauce and serve immediately, sprinkling the pepper over each individual portion after dishing out. You may serve additional Parmesan at the table.

NOTE: Once the noodles are cooked, this dish may be assembled at the table using a chafing dish.

LINGUINE WITH WHITE CLAM SAUCE

36 fresh hard-shell clams (small)
4 tablespoons butter
4 tablespoons olive oil
1 clove garlic, peeled and crushed through a press
¼ teaspoon freshly ground black pepper
2 tablespoons finely chopped fresh parsley
½ teaspoon dried oregano
¼ cup dry white wine
1 teaspoon salt
1½ pounds linguine (similar to spaghetti, but flat rather than round)

1. Open the clams, cut out muscle, and discard the shells. Wash clams thoroughly in cold running water.

2. Melt the butter with 2 tablespoons of the olive oil in a small saucepan. Add crushed garlic, pepper, parsley, oregano, wine, and the washed clams. Cover and cook gently over low heat for 15 minutes.

3. While the sauce is cooking, bring 4 quarts of water to a boil in a large stockpot or saucepan. Add salt and 2 tablespoons olive oil, then the linguine. The linguine should be added a little at a time so that the water continues to boil. Cook exactly 8 minutes, then drain in a colander.

4. Transfer hot linguine to a serving dish or platter, pour hot sauce over, and serve immediately.

HOMEMADE RAVIOLI

You can buy many forms of pasta at the supermarket, take it home, boil, drain, and serve. But ravioli is a different story because it contains a moist meat or cheese filling. I have never tasted frozen ravioli that I liked—the dough is too thick and gummy and the filling is bland, while the sauce tastes something like thin tomato catsup. Good ravioli must be made at home.

RAVIOLI DOUGH

4 cups all-purpose flour
1 teaspoon salt
2 eggs
½ cup ice-cold water

1. Sift the flour and salt together into a bowl, then add the eggs and water and blend either by hand or with a pastry blender and form into a ball of dough. Adjust for excessive dryness or wetness by adding either a little water or a little flour.

2. Knead the dough either on a floured surface or in the large bowl of an electric mixer or food processor equipped with a dough hook. The dough should achieve a very smooth and elastic consistency. Let the dough stand at least 30 minutes after kneading.

MEAT FILLING FOR RAVIOLI

3 tablespoons butter
2 tablespoons very finely minced onion
2 cups cooked beef, ham, chicken, or veal, run through fine
    blade of meat grinder
½ cup grated Parmesan or Romano cheese
¼ cup dry white bread crumbs
¼ teaspoon freshly ground black pepper

1. Melt the butter in a skillet, add the minced onions, and simmer over low heat about 2 minutes to soften. Add the ground meat and cook, stirring, over medium heat 5 minutes.

2. Turn off heat; stir in grated cheese, bread crumbs, and pepper to blend. Transfer the filling to a bowl and allow it to cool.

CHEESE FILLING FOR RAVIOLI

2 cups ricotta or cottage cheese, drained
½ cup grated Parmesan cheese
¼ cup dry white bread crumbs
¼ teaspoon freshly ground black pepper

Combine all the ingredients in a bowl until well blended.

NOTE: Each of the filling recipes is sufficient for all the dough. If you wish to make both, double the amount of dough or halve each filling recipe.

ASSEMBLING AND PREPARING RAVIOLI

1. Divide the dough into two portions and work with one at a time. Using a large floured surface roll out the dough and stretch it until it is about ⅛ inch thick. Cut into 2-inch-wide strips and mark off 2-inch intervals down the center of half the strips, using a ruler.

2. Place a rounded teaspoon of filling at 2-inch intervals on a strip of dough and cover with a second strip, pressing the dough down around the filling so that the resulting appearance is one

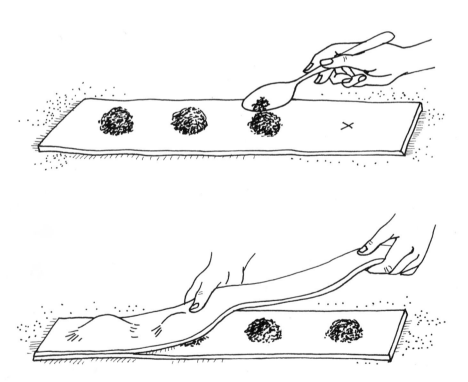

strip of dough with rounded bumps down the middle. Cut the dough into 2-inch squares, pressing down the edges to seal. Continue until all the dough and filling have been used. Let the finished ravioli squares stand and dry several hours before cooking. If you're preparing the ravioli a day early, they should go into the refrigerator right after making them; ravioli can also be frozen.

3. To cook, bring 6 quarts of water to a rolling boil in a large stockpot. Add 1 teaspoon salt and drop in the ravioli squares, about eight or ten at a time, and boil them 6 minutes or until the squares rise to the surface. Keep them warm while cooking the rest.

4. Drain and serve the ravioli hot with melted butter and grated Parmesan cheese. Ravioli may also be served with a rich tomato sauce or a meat sauce.

SPAGHETTI CARBONARA

In preparing this dish the important thing is timing. The spaghetti should be cooked, transferred to a colander, and drained just as the sauce is ready to add and toss. Avoid being forced to reheat the spaghetti after mixing in the sauce, because the egg yolks will tend to become gummy. I recommend about 8 minutes' cooking time for the spaghetti, and the sauce, if all the ingredients are measured and laid out beforehand, should take no more than 4 minutes.

2 tablespoons olive oil
1 teaspoon salt
2 pounds spaghetti
¼ pound butter
6 slices bacon, cut in thin strips
¼ pound boiled ham, sliced and cut into thin strips
4 egg yolks
¼ cup heavy cream
2 cups grated Parmesan cheese
    black pepper freshly ground in a pepper mill

1. Bring about 6 quarts of water to a boil in a large stockpot and add the olive oil, salt, and spaghetti. Time the cooking for 8 minutes *after* the water returns to a boil.

2. While the spaghetti is cooking, melt the butter in a skillet, add the strips of bacon and ham, and cook until the ham is lightly browned. Turn off heat.

3. Beat together the egg yolks, cream, and half the cheese in a bowl and have ready.

4. When the spaghetti is done, transfer immediately to drain for a few seconds in a large colander. Then slip the still-hot spaghetti into a warmed serving tureen, pour over the bacon and ham mixture directly from the skillet, toss, then add the cream/egg-yolk mixture, toss again, and finally sprinkle over the remaining cheese and a few turns of fresh black pepper from the mill. Serve immediately.

SPAGHETTI WITH MEATBALLS

Yes, you can bury the meatballs in tomato sauce and flood the spaghetti with the combination. But I prefer the taste of the meatballs, spaghetti, and Parmesan unobscured by tomatoes.

2 pounds fresh ground round of beef
¾ cup very finely chopped onion
¼ teaspoon freshly ground black pepper
   flour for dusting
4 tablespoons butter
1 cup beef broth *or* beef consommé
2 pounds spaghetti
1 teaspoon salt
3 tablespoons olive oil
1 cup freshly grated Parmesan cheese

1. Set about 6 quarts of cold water to boil in a large stockpot.

2. While the water is heating, knead together in a mixing bowl the ground beef, onion, and pepper. Then form the meat into balls about 1½ inches in diameter by rolling between your hands. Dust meatballs lightly with flour.

3. Melt the butter in a large cast-iron or enameled skillet and brown the meatballs on all sides in it. Add the beef broth to the pan, cover, and simmer 15 minutes.

4. Add the salt and olive oil to the boiling water, add the spaghetti, and cook for 8 minutes after it returns to a full boil, then drain in a colander.

5. Place the drained spaghetti on a large serving platter or dish, pour over it the meatballs with all their liquid, sprinkle generously with Parmesan cheese, and serve.

IV

Fish and Shellfish

POACHED WHOLE BASS OR SALMON

This recipe requires a fish poacher, a 4- to 5-inch-deep, 6-inch-wide, and about 18- to 20-inch-long vessel equipped with a platform for lifting out the fish after cooking without breaking it. Fish poachers come in a variety of materials and sizes, with solid tin-lined copper the most expensive, ranging down through aluminum and steel to ordinary white enamel. I find the inexpensive enamel type perfectly adequate and consider the others to be more for show than for practicality. The main point is that poaching a whole fish preserves the flavor, almost completely

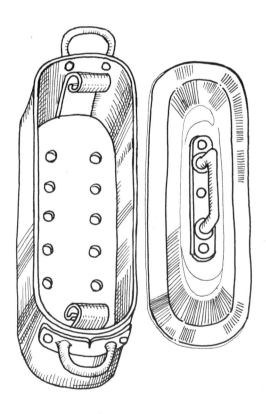

excludes the use of any fat, avoids dryness, which is often a problem in broiling or frying fish, and offers the opportunity for serving interesting and tasty sauces. The poacher is a very worthwhile investment.

1 4-pound whole bass or salmon (or other fish), cleaned with head and tail left on
2 tablespoons butter, softened
1 teaspoon salt
½ teaspoon freshly ground white pepper
1 cup chopped onion
2 large carrots, peeled and chopped
2 stalks celery, chopped
1 bay leaf
2 strips hickory-smoked bacon
4 bottles clam juice
1 cup dry white wine
½ cup white vinegar

1. Wash the fish in cold running water and pat dry inside and out. Butter the skin with the softened butter on both sides and place in fish poacher. Sprinkle with the salt and pepper.

2. Place the chopped onions, carrots, celery, bay leaf, and bacon strips inside the cavity.

3. Add the clam juice, wine, and vinegar to the poacher, pouring the liquids into a corner, not over the skin of the fish.

4. Turn oven on to 350 degrees, then place poacher across two burners of the stove. Turn burners on medium low and bring the liquid to a simmer, uncovered, while the oven heats.

5. When liquid is simmering, transfer poacher, covered, to oven, set timer for 30 minutes, and cook until done. To test for

doneness, insert a fork into the thickest part of the flesh (over the center of the spine) and push aside to examine flesh. It should *not* flake, but should be cooked through with an even texture and color close to the bone. If flesh near the bone is still raw, which would be apparent because the color differs from the cooked outer flesh, continue cooking for 10 more minutes and check again.

6. To serve, lift platform out of poacher carefully and slide fish onto a warm serving platter. Remove any remaining onion, celery, and other ingredients from the cavity. Strain the cooking liquid and use as thin broth-type gravy, or use broth as a base for making other sauces some other time. Fish may also be served with Hollandaise Sauce (see pages 160–61) or melted butter.

CODFISH CAKES NEW ENGLAND STYLE

2 pounds fresh codfish
8 medium-size boiling potatoes
3 eggs
1 tablespoon grated onion
½ teaspoon seasoned salt
¼ teaspoon freshly ground white pepper
3 tablespoons heavy cream
1 tablespoon butter for greasing baking dish

1. Place the piece of cod in a saucepan in enough cold water to cover by about ½ inch. Bring to a boil, reduce heat to produce a simmer, cover, and cook 20 minutes.

2. Peel and boil the potatoes in salted water until tender. Drain, mash, and place them in the bowl of an electric mixer.

3. Preheat oven to 350 degrees.

4. When the cod is done remove it from the water, drain, remove all skin and bones, and flake the meat into the bowl with the mashed potatoes.

5. Start the mixer at medium speed and add the eggs, one at a time, the grated onion, seasonings, and finally the cream. Continue beating until all ingredients are well blended and the texture of the mixture is fairly smooth.

6. Grease a large baking pan or ovenproof dish (or two smaller ones), form the mixture into patties about ¾ inch thick and 3 inches in diameter, arrange them in the pan, and bake 40 minutes. Serve hot.

GEFILTE FISH

This Jewish classic is normally served as a cold appetizer with grated horseradish (to be applied sparingly). Many people who enjoy it always buy it ready-made in the mistaken assumption that it is too difficult to prepare at home. Please try!

1 4- to 5-pound carp, cleaned, with head and tail left on
1 2- to 3-pound pike, cleaned, with head and tail left on
4 large stalks celery
1 pound onions, peeled
1 teaspoon salt
¼ teaspoon freshly ground white pepper
5 eggs, well beaten
4 large carrots, peeled and cut into quarters lengthwise
1 root fresh horseradish, scraped and grated, *or* 1 jar grated
   horseradish

1. Fillet the fish, retaining bones, heads, tails, and scraps. If you prefer, have the fish market do this step for you, but make sure you get all the scraps and bones.

2. Run the fillets through the finest blade of a meat grinder into a bowl, then do the same with the celery and onions.

3. Add salt and pepper and the beaten eggs to the fish, celery, and onions. Mix by hand until all the ingredients are well blended and there is an even texture throughout.

4. Arrange the fish scraps, bones, heads, and tails in the bottom of a large stockpot, fish poacher, or saucepan. Add the carrots. Cover with water by about ½ inch and bring to a boil.

5. While water is heating, form the fish mixture into oblong oval patties about 3 inches long and 1 inch thick. Wrap each one in one thickness of cheesecloth, tightly securing the cloth with toothpicks or stainless metal pins.

6. Using tongs, place the wrapped patties in the pot on the bones and scraps; cover, reduce heat, and cook 25 minutes at a slow simmer.

7. When done, remove patties with tongs and allow them to cool at room temperature, then carefully take off the cheesecloth. Meanwhile, remove large scraps from the cooking liquid, then strain the liquid through a very fine strainer into a shallow dish.

8. Place the unwrapped patties in the liquid and refrigerate. The liquid should become a soft gelatin. If you had very few bones or no bones in the original cooking liquid, then you should dissolve 1 envelope of unflavored gelatin powder in a little of the liquid, add it to the main body, and simmer, then cool before using.

9. Serve the gefilte fish chilled with the gelatin, garnished with grated horseradish.

MARINATED PERCH

1 tablespoon thinly sliced scallions
½ cup minced celery
½ cup finely chopped carrots
½ cup liquefied or grated onion
¼ cup (4 tablespoons) olive oil
1 cup dry white wine
¼ cup white vinegar
1 bay leaf
1 teaspoon grated lemon rind
6 medium-size perch, cleaned
½ teaspoon salt
¼ teaspoon freshly ground white pepper
½ cup flour

1. In a small saucepan cook the scallion, celery, carrots, and onion in 2 tablespoons of the oil for 3 or 4 minutes over medium heat without browning.

2. Add the wine, vinegar, bay leaf, and lemon rind; cover, bring to a simmer, and cook about 20 minutes.

3. Dry the fish well, mix the salt and pepper with the flour, then dust the fish with this mixture.

4. Heat the remaining 2 tablespoons oil in a large skillet and fry the fish to a golden brown on both sides.

5. Arrange the fried fish in a shallow dish just large enough to fit them all in one layer. Pour the hot marinade over the perch, then let it cool to room temperature. Serve cool but not chilled.

FRESH FRIED SMELTS

When smelts are in season there are few fish that can match them in taste and delicacy. They are very easy to prepare and if there is any pitfall to avoid it is overcooking.

18 medium-size fresh smelts, cleaned, with heads and tails left on
½ cup flour
½ teaspoon salt
¼ teaspoon freshly ground black pepper
4 tablespoons good-quality olive oil *or* vegetable shortening
4 tablespoons butter

1. Wash the smelts carefully under cold running water, then pat them dry with paper towels.

2. Roll them in a mixture of the flour, salt, and pepper.

3. Heat the oil in a heavy skillet, then add the butter and allow it to melt. Quickly place the smelts in the skillet, fry to a golden brown on one side, turn, do the same for the other side, remove, and serve hot.

4. Smelts may be served on toast and should be garnished with lemon wedges and tartar sauce.

TARTAR SAUCE

1½ cups mayonnaise
2 teaspoons hot English mustard

2 teaspoons finely minced onion
1 tablespoon finely chopped pickle
1 teaspoon white vinegar

Combine all ingredients and keep refrigerated until serving time.

FILLETS OF SOLE AMANDINE

This is a simple, delicious, and easy-to-serve main course with only one small drawback when it comes to serving it to six people: having a sufficiently large frying surface. I use a flat cast-aluminum griddle that sits over two adjacent burners on the stove. The griddle is equipped with a gutter all around to catch excess fat.

6 fillets of sole (you may use Boston sole, gray sole, flounder, or any similar fish)
2 eggs
1 pint milk
8 tablespoons (¼-pound stick) butter
1 cup white slivered almonds
4 tablespoons best-quality French olive oil

1. At least 1 hour before preparation place the fillets in a shallow dish and pour over them a mixture of the eggs beaten in the milk. Let them soak in the refrigerator until you are ready to cook.

2. Preheat the oven to about 250 degrees and place in it a large serving platter.

3. Melt 4 tablespoons of the butter in a small frying pan, add the slivered almonds, and cook until the almonds are golden brown, stirring often. Remove from heat and set aside.

4. Place the griddle over the burners and heat until a drop of water released on the surface bounces.

5. Melt 2 tablespoons of butter on the surface, add 2 tablespoons olive oil, then quickly lay onto the griddle three of the fillets. It is not necessary to drain off the milk mixture; the fish should be as wet as possible when placed on the cooking surface. Fry the fish 3 minutes on the first side, turn once, and fry 2 minutes on the second side. I recommend using a large spatula to pick up the fillet and a second, smaller spatula to hold it flat while turning. When done, transfer the cooked fillets to the warm platter in the oven and cook the other three in the same manner.

6. When all six are done, immediately pour the browned almonds and butter sauce over them and serve.

FILLETS OF SOLE BONNE FEMME

Although this recipe is a bit long, it is not at all complicated to prepare, does not require a great deal of time, and the results are well worth your effort. It is especially important to measure and lay out the ingredients in advance to avoid having to stop in the middle to find a missing item.

6 fillets of sole (or similar fish)
¼ cup fresh lemon juice
1¼ teaspoons salt
½ teaspoon freshly ground white pepper
9 fresh, firm medium-size mushrooms
½ pound butter (approximately)
¾ cup white wine
½ cup clam juice
6 tablespoons flour
1 pinch cayenne pepper
¾ cup half and half (½ milk, ½ cream)
¼ cup heavy cream
3 egg yolks, well beaten

1. Wash the fillets of sole in cold water and lemon juice, reserving 4 teaspoons of lemon juice for use later. Pat them dry, fold them once lengthwise, and lay them in a buttered ovenproof baking dish. Sprinkle the fillets with ¼ teaspoon salt and ⅛ teaspoon white pepper. Preheat oven to 350 degrees.

2. Chop three of the mushrooms fine. Melt 2 tablespoons butter in a small saucepan, add the chopped mushrooms, shake pan to coat them with butter, add 2 teaspoons lemon juice and ¼ teaspoon pepper, and simmer 1 minute.

3. Add the white wine and clam juice and bring to a boil. As soon as the boil is reached pour the contents of the saucepan over the fillets of sole in the baking dish and put it into the preheated oven for 12 minutes.

4. While the sole fillets are cooking, melt 6 tablespoons butter in a saucepan over low heat, stir in 6 tablespoons flour, ¾ teaspoon salt, and the cayenne and mix until smooth, cooking for at least 2 minutes over medium heat. Turn off heat.

5. When the fish are done carefully remove them to a shallow oval gratin dish and keep them warm. Then strain the liquid from

the baking dish into the sauce mixture, turn on a medium flame, and stir until the liquid is incorporated into the sauce and it thickens. Stir in the half and half and the heavy cream and continue to cook over a low flame until the sauce barely starts to simmer at the edges. Turn off heat and beat in the egg yolks with a wire whisk until well blended. Remove sauce from heat, cover, and set aside.

6. Slice the remaining six mushrooms very thin and cook them in 5 tablespoons melted butter in a small skillet. Add 2 teaspoons lemon juice, ¼ teaspoon salt, and ⅛ teaspoon pepper and cook about 3 minutes, stirring often. Turn off heat and set aside.

7. Turn on oven broiler to high. Using a slotted spoon scatter the sliced mushrooms over the fillets of sole, then cover with the prepared sauce. At this point you should be almost ready to serve the main course.

8. Place the gratin dish under the broiler, keeping the door open and watching the whole time. When the surface of the sauce turns a golden brown color (it takes only a few seconds) with patches of darker brown, remove from broiler and serve immediately.

GRILLED SWORDFISH STEAKS WITH BÉARNAISE SAUCE

This dish is very simple to prepare but requires the correct equipment. Indispensable: a heavy cast-iron or aluminum stove-top grill with raised ridges and run-off well, of the size that fits over two burners. For the sauce: an ovenproof glass double boiler, minimum 1½-quart capacity, and a wire whisk.

BÉARNAISE SAUCE

4 egg yolks
1 tablespoon plus 1 teaspoon lemon juice
12 tablespoons (1½ sticks) butter
¼ teaspoon salt
1 tablespoon tarragon vinegar
1 teaspoon chopped fresh tarragon *or* ½ teaspoon dried tarragon
1 teaspoon chopped fresh chervil *or* ½ teaspoon dried chervil
1 teaspoon chopped fresh parsley *or* ½ teaspoon dried parsley

1. Heat about 2 inches of water in the lower vessel of the double boiler to a simmer, then reduce heat to medium low. The water should *not* be boiling.

2. Beat the egg yolks well in a small bowl, add the lemon juice, and place handy to the stove.

3. Put one-third of the butter (½ stick) into the top vessel of the double boiler over the hot water, immediately add the egg yolk and lemon mixture, and beat with the wire whisk.

4. When the first piece of butter has completely melted, add the next one-third of the butter and continue beating. Do not stop beating for more than a moment during the entire process of incorporating the butter.

5. In the same manner add the last piece of butter and continue beating until the butter is melted and the sauce thickens considerably.

6. *Off heat* add the salt, vinegar, and herbs, stir well, cover the sauce, and let it stand at room temperature until ready to transfer to sauce boat and serve. *Do not* place on warming tray or any kind of heat source.

SWORDFISH STEAKS

6 1-inch-thick swordfish steaks, fresh, *or* well thawed if frozen
2 tablespoons olive oil
½ teaspoon paprika
6 lemon wedges

1. Heat the grill for a few minutes before cooking so that a drop of water bounces and rolls when released on the surface.

2. Brush both sides of the steaks with olive oil and sprinkle with paprika.

3. Grill for 3 minutes on each side. Loosen carefully with a spatula before turning to avoid tearing and sticking. Just before turning, brush a little more oil on top of each steak.

4. Serve hot with the Béarnaise Sauce and garnish with lemon wedges.

TRUITE AU BLEU

In my humble opinion this is absolutely the best way to prepare and serve fresh trout. The ideal is to use live trout, bring the water to a boil, eviscerate the trout with one stroke of a sharp knife followed by one quick plunge with a crooked finger to remove the intestines, and immediately immerse the fish in the water. Trout prepared this way in the great restaurants of Europe comes to the table slightly twisted as evidence of its freshness. In the absence of live trout, however, you may use a frozen one with almost equal results provided it was flash frozen when very fresh. The same technique may be used for any fairly small freshwater whole fish.

6 live trout, *or* fresh frozen trout, heads and tails left on, but eviscerated
3 cups white vinegar
¾ cup butter, melted
6 sprigs parsley
6 lemon wedges

1. Bring about 4 quarts of water to a boil in a fish poacher or large stockpot, to a depth of at least 4 inches.

2. Clean the trout quickly if not already done.

3. Add the vinegar to the water, let it return to the boil, drop in the trout. Boil exactly 5 minutes if trout are fresh, 6 minutes if frozen.

4. Immediately remove trout from the water, drain a few seconds on paper towels, transfer to a warm serving platter or individual plates, pour melted butter over, garnish with parsley and lemon, and serve hot.

NOTE: Traditionally Truite au Bleu is served with tiny boiled potatoes.

WHITING BAKED WITH WINE

6 medium to small whiting (⅓ to ½ pound each)
2 tablespoons finely minced onion
2 tablespoons finely minced celery
¼ cup butter, melted
½ cup dry white wine
¼ cup white vinegar
¼ teaspoon salt
¼ teaspoon freshly ground white pepper
3 tablespoons chopped parsley
3 tablespoons dry bread crumbs *or* matzo meal
4 tablespoons butter, softened

1. Preheat oven to 350 degrees.

2. Clean the whiting, slash sides with a very sharp knife, two cuts on each side of each fish, or have your fish market prepare them.

3. Sprinkle the bottom of a shallow ovenproof baking dish with the onions and celery, then pour in the melted butter.

4. Arrange the fish in the dish. Pour the wine and vinegar over the fish, then sprinkle on the salt and pepper. Mix the parsley with the bread crumbs in a little bowl and sprinkle this mixture over the fish.

5. Dot the surface with softened butter, bake 30 minutes uncovered in the preheated oven, and serve hot.

STEAMED ALASKA KING CRAB LEGS

Unless you live in Alaska or perhaps Washington State you will have to use frozen King Crab legs. Thaw them before starting the recipe.

3 pounds frozen Alaska King Crab legs
2 cups butter, melted
   seasoned salt
2 cups bottled clam juice
½ cup dry white wine
2 tablespoons grated onion
6 peppercorns, cracked

1. Slit the thawed crab legs lengthwise and spoon melted butter into the leg meat until well saturated. Sprinkle meat with a little seasoned salt.

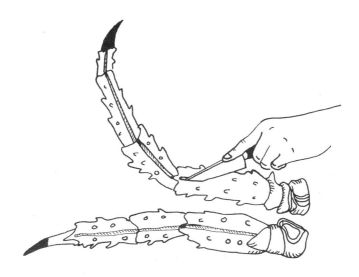

2. Combine clam juice, wine, grated onion, and peppercorns in a saucepan. Add a steamer platform or raised rack, and arrange the prepared crab legs over the liquid.

3. Bring to a boil, cover, and steam 7 minutes. Remove the legs with tongs to a serving platter. Strain the broth. Serve the legs hot with a small cup of the broth and the remaining melted butter.

STEAMED CLAMS WITH DRAWN BUTTER

In the Northeast it is traditional to use the Long Island–type steamer clams with long necks for this dish. However, any kind of clams may be prepared in the same way. I recommend using a large, two-sectioned clam steamer for this recipe. The lower section should have a spigot.

6 quarts fresh clams in their shells
1 pound butter

1. Scrub the clams under cold running water, cutting away any protruding beards with a small, sharp paring knife.

2. Bring 1 quart of water to a boil in the lower vessel of the steamer. Put the clams in the upper vessel, cover, and steam for at least 20 minutes, or until all the clams have opened.

3. While the clams are steaming, melt the butter in a saucepan over a low flame. Pour off clear butter, leaving behind the milky white residue in the pan.

4. Discard any unopened clams. Serve hot clams with a small cup of butter and a cup of the juice from the lower vessel of the steamer for each person for dipping. For tyros, the clam, held by the long tail, should be dipped first in the broth to remove any remaining sand, then into the butter.

FRIED SOFT-SHELL CRABS WITH TARTAR SAUCE

Have your fish market clean the soft-shell crabs for you and make sure you cook them the same day. If you must do the job yourself, the procedure is to cut out the face from behind the eyes, then remove the gills and sandbag from the underbelly and the small triangular apron at the bottom of the shell. The season for this delicacy is short because it lasts only from the time the crab has molted until its new shell hardens.

24 soft-shell crabs (cleaned)
4 to 6 cups vegetable oil *or* shortening for deep frying
1 cup all-purpose flour
3 eggs, beaten
3 tablespoons milk
2 cups fine white bread crumbs

1. Wash the crabs under cold running water, then dry thoroughly with paper towels.

2. Heat frying oil in deep fryer to 375 degrees. Use a fat thermometer if your fryer has no thermostat.

3. Dust each crab with flour so that a very light coating adheres. Then dip in a mixture of the beaten eggs and milk, and finally roll in the bread crumbs to produce an even coating. Lower into the hot fat and fry about 5 minutes or until golden brown. Do not do more than three or four crabs at a time. Transfer the fried crabs to a platter lined with paper towels in a warm oven until all are done.

4. Serve hot with Tartar Sauce (see page 80).

CRAB STEW

2 pounds cooked lump crab meat
¾ cup sherry *or* light Madeira wine
3 tablespoons butter
½ cup finely minced shallots
¼ cup finely minced pimiento
2 tablespoons flour
¼ teaspoon dried chervil
½ cup tomato paste
½ teaspoon salt
¼ teaspoon freshly ground white pepper
1¼ cups half and half (½ milk, ½ cream) *or* light cream

1. Remove all bits of cartilage and shell from the crab meat. Place it in a bowl, packed down tightly, and pour the wine over it. Marinate at least 1 hour at room temperature.

2. In a medium-size saucepan melt the butter over low heat, then cook the shallots and pimientos in the butter for 3 or 4 minutes until shallots are soft and transparent.

3. Add the flour, stir well, and cook 2 more minutes. Add the chervil, tomato paste, salt, and pepper and bring to a simmer.

4. Now add the crab meat with all the liquid in the bowl, then the half and half. Bring the stew to a slow simmer, stirring, and do not allow it to boil. Serve hot over a bed of rice.

LOBSTER FRA DIAVOLO

If you agree that it is not necessary to display courage in the privacy of your kitchen, especially when nobody will ever know, have your fishmonger prepare your lobsters according to your instructions and avoid the risk of chopping off your own fingers!

¾ cup olive oil
6 1- to 1½-pound lobsters, with claws chopped from bodies and
    cracked, bodies split in half with veins and sacs removed
4 cloves garlic, peeled and cut in half
½ cup brandy *or* cognac
8 large tomatoes, peeled, seeded, and chopped
2 teaspoons seasoned salt
¼ teaspoon cayenne pepper
1 teaspoon dried oregano
3 tablespoons finely minced onion
3 tablespoons chopped parsley
¾ cup clam juice

1. In a large casserole heat the olive oil, then add the lobster pieces, with the flesh side of the tail sections down, and the cut

garlic. Cook over medium heat, uncovered, until the garlic has browned, then remove the garlic.

2. Add the brandy and light it with a match. When the flames die out add the tomatoes, seasonings, onion, parsley, and clam juice; cover and cook 25 minutes more.

3. Serve the lobster piping hot, in soup plates, providing small lobster forks in addition to regular cutlery. I advise large napkins or bibs!

SAUTÉED SCALLOPS IN WINE AND SHALLOTS

1½ pounds fresh sea scallops, cleaned and cut in half if very large
¼ cup flour
6 tablespoons butter
½ teaspoon salt
¼ teaspoon freshly ground white pepper
1 cup dry white wine
½ cup minced fresh shallots *or* frozen shallots, thawed and minced fine
1 tablespoon fresh chopped parsley *or* 2 teaspoons dried parsley flakes
6 lemon wedges

1. Wash the scallops in cold water, pat dry with paper towels.

2. Dust the scallops with flour. Melt the butter in a large skillet equipped with a cover. Sauté the dusted scallops in the butter, turning frequently until slightly browned to a golden color on all sides.

3. Sprinkle with salt and pepper, add wine, shallots, and parsley to the skillet, reduce heat to medium low, cover, and simmer for about 15 minutes, stirring occasionally.

4. Serve immediately with rice and garnish with lemon wedges.

SHRIMP IN LOBSTER AND DILL SAUCE

This recipe requires a product called lobster paste, which comes in small cans of about 4-ounce capacity and can be found in gourmet shops, oriental food shops, and well-stocked delicatessens. The paste is made from edible leftover parts of lobsters, the tail and claw meat of which has been processed for canning or freezing.

2 pounds fresh shrimp, medium size
¼ cup lemon juice
1 bay leaf
10 black peppercorns, cracked
6 tablespoons butter
6 tablespoons flour
2 4-ounce cans lobster paste
½ cup finely chopped fresh dill *or* ¼ cup dried dill weed
2 cups bottled clam juice
2 teaspoons Maggi liquid seasoning *or* Worcestershire sauce
½ cup sherry

1. Peel, clean, and wash the shrimp under cold running water.

2. Bring 4 quarts of water to a boil in a large saucepan or stock-pot. Add the lemon juice, bay leaf, and peppercorns to the water, and lower the shrimp into the water in a colander or a large sieve. Boil 5 minutes exactly and lift out immediately. Allow the shrimp to cool at room temperature while preparing the sauce.

3. Melt the butter in a double boiler over simmering water, add the flour, stir into a paste, and cook for 3 minutes, stirring. Stir in lobster paste and chopped dill.

4. Add the clam juice a little at a time, stirring constantly, until sauce achieves desired consistency, which should be that of thick gravy. Stir in seasoning and sherry, and add a little boiling water if sauce is still too thick.

5. Place the cooked shrimp in the sauce and allow them to heat through over slightly simmering water for at least 15 minutes. At this point the upper vessel of the double boiler may be removed from the lower one and placed on a hot tray or other warming surface, or it may be refrigerated for later reheating.

6. Serve the shrimp in the sauce, piping hot, over rice.

BOUILLABAISSE

This is a main-course dish which is often served in a large soup plate to accommodate plenty of shellfish and save the delicious broth. I strongly advise either a very informal setting for this meal or at least the provision of lobster bibs or large napkins tucked in at the collar to protect clothing.

10 pounds assorted white ocean fish, including 1 live lobster. The fish should be cleaned and filleted at the fish market. Make sure you get all scraps, heads, tails, and bones plus some extras if possible.

2 cups chopped onion

½ cup olive oil

⅔ cup tomato paste

3 cloves garlic, peeled and crushed through a press

2 cups bottled clam juice

2 teaspoons salt

½ teaspoon freshly ground black pepper

4 tablespoons minced parsley

1 bay leaf

¼ teaspoon thyme

1 teaspoon saffron

12 mussels *or* clams (fresh in shells)

1. Cut the pieces of fish into 1- to 2-inch pieces and set aside from scraps and bones. Chop the lobster into 2-inch pieces, adding central body to scraps after setting aside tail and claw pieces.

2. In a large 5- to 6-quart-capacity saucepan soften the onions in the oil over a medium flame for a few minutes without browning. Then add the tomato paste and garlic and continue stirring and cooking for 3 or 4 more minutes.

3. Pour in 2½ quarts cold water, the clam juice, salt, pepper, parsley, bay leaf, thyme, and saffron. Finally add all the *scraps* of fish and lobster. Bring to a boil.

4. After boiling 15 minutes turn off heat and strain the soup into another container. Discard scraps.

5. Rinse out the large saucepan, return strained soup to it, and bring to a boil. Now add the pieces of fish, lobster, and the mussels. Boil 6 minutes. Discard any mussels that do not open.

6. Serve in soup plates, distributing various items as evenly as possible, then pouring liquid over. The perfect accompaniment is a hot crusty loaf of garlic bread and a cold bottle of dry white wine.

ENGLISH FISH AND CHIPS

vegetable oil for deep frying
2 pounds fillets from any lean white fish
2 eggs
¾ cup milk
1 teaspoon seasoned salt
2 cups fine bread crumbs *or* cracker crumbs *or* matzo meal

1. Heat oil in a deep fryer to 375 degrees. Use a fat thermometer if your fryer is not equipped with a thermostat.

2. While oil is heating, cut the fish into 1-inch cubes, wash the pieces of fish, then dry them thoroughly with paper towels. It is very important to remove all water to prevent spattering in the oil.

3. Dip the pieces of fish in a mixture of the eggs beaten with the milk.

4. Sprinkle a little salt over the fish, then roll them in the bread crumbs until they are completely coated with a thin layer. Prepare all the pieces of fish and lay them out on a board or platter handy to the fryer before starting to cook.

5. Place a platter in the oven, setting temperature at about 250 degrees to keep fish warm after frying.

6. Place only enough fish cubes in the basket of your fryer to form one layer. Lower the basket into the hot oil and fry until golden brown, about 4 to 5 minutes. Shake basket occasionally to prevent sticking. When the first batch is done, place the pieces on paper towels to drain for a few seconds, then transfer to warm platter in the oven. Continue process until all the fish is cooked.

7. Serve hot with French-Fried Potatoes (see page 166) and Tartar Sauce (page 80).

PAELLA MARINARA

1 small to medium-size lobster, cooked
1 pound raw shrimp, peeled and deveined
1 2-pound chicken, cut into serving pieces
¼ teaspoon freshly ground black pepper
1 teaspoon salt
1 clove garlic, peeled and crushed through a press
½ cup olive oil
2 teaspoons red wine vinegar
1 cup sliced garlic sausage
6 slices bacon, cut into 1-inch strips
1 cup chopped onion
½ cup chopped fresh green pepper
½ cup tomato paste
2 cups uncooked white rice
1 teaspoon saffron
2 dozen cherrystone clams in their shells, scrubbed

1. Crack the lobster and remove the meat. Cut it into bite-size pieces and set aside.

2. Drop the shrimp into about 3 quarts of boiling water, boil 5 minutes, remove from water, and drain.

3. Pat dry the chicken pieces. Using a large paella pan or deep, heavy enameled saucepan, combine the pepper, salt, garlic, and oil; heat, add chicken pieces, and cook them to brown on all sides.

4. Add the vinegar, sausage, bacon strips, onion, and green pepper; stir and cook 10 minutes.

5. Add tomato paste, rice, and saffron and stir until simmering; then add 4 cups water, turn heat to high, and bring to a boil. Reduce heat, cover, and cook 15 to 20 minutes until liquid is absorbed by the rice.

6. During step 5, steam the clams in a covered saucepan with about 1 inch of water in the bottom until they open (discard any that do not open). Turn off heat.

7. Stir the rice with the other ingredients in the pot from bottom to top to mix them, then add clams with their liquid to the pot, and the lobster and shrimps. Cover and cook just long enough to absorb additional liquid. Turn off heat and serve immediately.

V

Poultry

BREASTS OF CHICKEN WITH BUTTER SAUCE

6 whole chicken breasts
8 tablespoons butter
3 tablespoons fresh lemon juice
¾ teaspoon freshly ground white pepper
2 tablespoons finely minced shallots
⅓ cup dry white wine
⅓ cup white wine vinegar
½ teaspoon salt
1 pound unsalted butter
2 tablespoons fresh chopped parsley

1. Remove skin and bones from chicken breasts, split them in half, and pound each of the twelve pieces flat with the side of a cleaver. This may be done between two sheets of waxed paper to avoid sticking. Melt the butter. Preheat oven to 400 degrees.

2. Butter the bottom of a large ovenproof baking dish equipped with a cover. If there is no cover, cut a double thickness of waxed paper or aluminum foil to fit. Arrange the chicken breasts in the dish, sprinkle with the lemon juice and ½ teaspoon pepper, and pour the melted butter over them, wetting all the exposed surfaces. Bake in the preheated oven, covered, for 10 minutes.

3. While chicken is baking, simmer the shallots, wine, vinegar, salt, and ¼ teaspoon pepper in a small enameled saucepan for about 3 minutes. While this is simmering, cut up the 1 pound of unsalted butter into approximately 1-tablespoon pieces. After the 3 minutes, reduce heat to low and add about six pieces of butter to the pan, stirring well until they melt. Now mix the

sauce with a hand-held mixer at medium to low speed, adding the rest of the butter a few pieces at a time, until all has been incorporated.

4. The chicken breasts should be ready just about when the sauce is completed. Lay the breasts out on a warm serving platter, pour the sauce over them, sprinkle with the chopped parsley, and serve immediately.

CHICKEN IN CHEESE CASSEROLE

2 3- to 4-pound fryers, cut into serving pieces
1 teaspoon salt
½ teaspoon freshly ground white pepper
8 tablespoons (¼-pound stick) butter
4 tablespoons flour
½ cup chicken broth *or* chicken consommé
1 cup half and half (½ milk, ½ cream) *or* light cream
½ cup grated Parmesan cheese
½ cup grated Swiss cheese
4 egg yolks, beaten
2 tablespoons Worcestershire sauce
¼ cup Madeira wine

1. Preheat oven to 350 degrees.

2. Rub the chicken pieces with the salt and pepper. Melt 4 tablespoons butter in a large skillet, brown the chicken pieces on both sides, cover the skillet, and cook the chicken over medium-low heat for 20 minutes until just tender.

3. In a large saucepan melt the remaining butter, add the flour, and stir into a smooth paste. Cook 2 minutes, stirring. Add the chicken broth a little at a time, stirring constantly, then the half and half, producing a fairly thick sauce.

4. Stir in ¼ cup of Parmesan and ¼ cup of Swiss cheese, then beat in the egg yolks with a wire whisk, followed by the Worcestershire sauce and the Madeira.

5. In a shallow casserole big enough to hold all the chicken, sprinkle half the remaining cheese on the bottom, put the cooked chicken pieces on the cheese, and pour the sauce over, coating all the pieces of chicken. Sprinkle the rest of the cheese over the top and bake in the preheated oven for 10 minutes.

OPTIONAL: Place the casserole under the oven broiler to brown surface just before serving.

CHICKEN CÔTELETTES

4 pounds chicken breasts, boned and skinned (It is very impor-
    tant that the meat be weighed *after* boning and skinning;
    otherwise the quantity will be insufficient for six people.)
½ cup very finely chopped onion (almost a puree)
2 cups cubed white bread, crusts removed
1 cup chicken broth
½ cup melted butter
1 tablespoon Worcestershire sauce
½ teaspoon salt
½ teaspoon freshly ground white pepper
1 cup flour for dredging
4 to 6 tablespoons vegetable shortening *or* oil for frying

1. Run the boned chicken breasts through the fine blade of the meat grinder or have the butcher do it for you, making sure he cleans any *beef* out of his grinder before starting.

2. In a large bowl, using bare hands or a heavy wooden spoon, combine the ground chicken with the chopped onion. Soak the bread cubes in a combination of the chicken broth, melted butter, and Worcestershire sauce, then work them into the meat mixture. Sprinkle salt and pepper over the meat and knead until well blended. Refrigerate the mixture for 1 hour.

3. Form the mixture into balls about 1½ inches in diameter and dredge them in flour to form a thin coating.

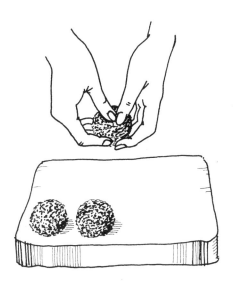

4. Heat about one-third of the shortening in a heavy cast-iron skillet, add some of the balls, and fry them about 5 minutes on each side until golden brown and cooked through but not dried out.

5. As you finish the first batch, add some shortening to the pan before continuing, and cut through one côtelette to make sure it is cooked through. Transfer the finished côtelettes to a warm platter and serve as soon as possible.

6. These côtelettes are excellent cold and may be sliced for sandwiches or hors d'oeuvres. They may also be reheated by placing them in an ovenproof dish, adding some cream or broth, and baking at 325 degrees for about 20 minutes or until the liquid in the dish is simmering.

CHICKEN CROQUETTES

breasts of 3 fryers, boned and skinned
3 eggs, separated
2 tablespoons butter, softened
¼ cup milk
½ cup white bread crumbs
¾ cup finely chopped mushrooms
¼ cup finely minced onion
½ teaspoon seasoned salt
¼ teaspoon freshly ground white pepper
¾ cup toasted bread crumbs
4 tablespoons vegetable shortening

1. Run the chicken breasts through the finest blade of a meat grinder or have the butcher grind the chicken for you.

2. Beat the egg yolks with the softened butter, add to the ground meat, and blend thoroughly, using your hands.

3. Add the milk to the white bread crumbs, stir, then add this moist mixture to the meat and mix well. In the same way work in the chopped mushrooms and onions until all the ingredients are evenly distributed. Season with salt and pepper.

4. Beat the egg whites until they form stiff peaks. Fold them into the meat mixture gently.

5. Form the meat into round patties about 2 inches in diameter and 1 inch thick. This recipe should produce about 1 dozen. Roll them in the toasted bread crumbs and arrange them handy to your cooking surface. Preheat oven to 375 degrees.

6. Heat the shortening in a large skillet and fry the croquettes on both sides until golden brown. Transfer them to an ovenproof dish as they are done.

7. Bake the croquettes 6 minutes in the preheated oven just before serving.

NOTE: A tomato, mushroom, Hollandaise, cream, or other sauce may be served but is not necessary, because the croquettes should be moist and tender inside.

CURRIED CHICKEN

2 5- to 5½-pound stewing chickens
1 large onion, peeled and cut in quarters
3 stalks celery, chopped
3 large carrots, peeled and chopped
6 peppercorns, cracked
1 cup very finely minced onion
¼ pound butter
5 tablespoons curry powder
½ cup flour
¼ cup heavy cream
2 tablespoons fresh chopped parsley
½ teaspoon seasoned salt
2 teaspoons lemon juice
1 teaspoon sugar
1 teaspoon Worcestershire sauce

1. Wash and clean the chickens. Place them in a large stewing pot or stockpot with 2 quarts of water, the onion quarters, celery, carrots, and peppercorns and bring to a simmer. Remove any scum that forms on top of the liquid, and continue simmering, uncovered, for about 2 hours until chickens are tender.

2. When done, remove chickens from the liquid and allow them to cool. Strain the broth and boil it down to about 1 quart.

3. When the chickens are cool enough to handle, use a sharp paring knife to remove all the meat from the bones, discarding skin, until you have a bowl of cooked chicken meat. Set aside.

4. In a medium-size saucepan, simmer the minced onions in the butter over a medium flame for several minutes until they are soft without having browned. Add the curry powder and the flour, stir well, and cook another 3 or 4 minutes. Add the quart

of broth, a little at a time, stirring well until you have a fairly thick sauce.

5. Reduce heat to just under the boiling point and add the cream, parsley, salt, lemon juice, sugar, and Worcestershire sauce. Taste the sauce frequently during this procedure and add more seasoning to taste if necessary.

6. Add the chicken meat to the sauce, stir, and heat only long enough to make sure the meat acquires the same temperature as the sauce.

7. Serve hot over rice, garnished with chutney.

CHICKEN FRICASSEE

A mild, easy-to-prepare, easy-to-serve dish very appropriate for buffet service.

2 stewing chickens, cleaned
2 teaspoons salt
1 teaspoon freshly ground white pepper
2 large onions, peeled and cut into chunks
2 large carrots, peeled and cut in half lengthwise
4 stalks celery, chopped
5 tablespoons butter
6 tablespoons flour
1 teaspoon seasoned salt
½ cup dry white wine

1. Rub the chickens with salt and pepper, and sprinkle a little of each in the cavities.

2. Place the chickens in a large stockpot with the onions, carrots, and celery. Cover them with cold water, bring to a boil, reduce heat to a simmer, cover, and cook 2 to 3 hours until chickens are tender but not overcooked.

3. Carefully remove chickens from the broth onto a working surface. Allow them to cool sufficiently to handle. Using a small, sharp paring knife, remove all skin and bones and place cooked meat in a bowl. Set aside.

4. Strain the cooking liquid and skim off the fat.

5. Melt the butter in a medium-size saucepan, add the flour and seasoned salt, and stir into a smooth paste. Cook 3 minutes, stirring, without allowing the paste to brown.

6. Add first the wine, then some of the broth, a little at a time, stirring constantly to form a smooth, fairly thick sauce. You should have about 2½ to 3 cups of sauce, and more if you make it thinner. Save any unused chicken broth for future use in soups or sauces.

7. Return the chicken meat to the sauce, heat through, and serve hot.

GRILLED MARINATED SPLIT BABY CHICKENS

3 baby fryers, cleaned and split in *half* only
1 cup olive oil
½ cup red wine vinegar
1 tablespoon soy sauce
2 teaspoons finely minced garlic, *or* 2 teaspoons dried garlic chips
½ teaspoon salt
½ teaspoon freshly ground black pepper
1 tablespoon minced parsley
2 teaspoons lemon juice
1 teaspoon Worcestershire sauce

1. Wash and pat dry and split baby chickens.

2. Combine all the remaining ingredients to make a marinade, and let stand at least 15 minutes, especially if you used dried garlic chips.

3. Arrange the chicken halves in a large, shallow ovenproof dish and pour the marinade over them, taking care to wet them thoroughly. Refrigerate the dish for 3 hours, basting the chickens with the marinade every half-hour and turning them over once halfway through.

4. Preheat oven to 325 degrees while chickens are marinating. Also preheat stove broiler if a separate unit.

5. Remove marinated chickens from refrigerator and let stand just long enough for the ovenproof dish to warm up to room temperature. Bake 30 minutes in preheated oven, basting occasionally.

6. Remove from oven and transfer chicken halves to broiler tray or to a stove-top grill. Reserve marinade liquid remaining.

7. Grill or broil on each side for about 4 minutes or until well browned, basting with the marinade. Serve immediately, using any remaining liquid as a sauce.

CHICKEN À LA KING

2 5- to 5½-pound stewing chickens
1 large onion, peeled and cut into quarters
3 stalks celery, chopped
3 large carrots, peeled and cut in half lengthwise
6 fresh medium-size mushrooms
12 tablespoons (1½ sticks) butter
¼ teaspoon freshly ground black pepper
6 tablespoons flour
2 cups chicken broth *or* chicken consommé
1 cup half and half (½ milk, ½ cream)
2 teaspoons Worcestershire sauce
½ teaspoon seasoned salt
½ cup canned pimientos

1. Wash and clean the chickens. Place them, with the onion, celery, and carrots, in a large stockpot with 2 quarts of water, bring to a boil, reduce heat to a simmer, cover, and cook about 2 hours until chickens are tender but not so done that the meat is falling off the bones.

2. Remove chickens from liquid, drain, let them cool, remove all skin and bones, and cut the meat into bite-size pieces. Re-

serve the cooked carrots and celery and cut these vegetables into bite-size pieces.

3. Slice the mushrooms into thin slices, melt 6 tablespoons of the butter in a skillet, and simmer the mushrooms in the butter, shaking the pan to coat them well and sprinkling them with the pepper, for 3 minutes. Remove from heat and set aside.

4. In a large saucepan over medium heat, melt the remaining 6 tablespoons butter, add the flour, and stir into a paste. Cook for 2 minutes. Now add the chicken broth, a little at a time, cooking and stirring constantly, and then the half and half. The texture should be that of fairly thick gravy. If still too thick add a little more chicken broth. NOTE: If the liquid in which the chickens were stewed has acquired enough taste, you may skim the surface and use some of it.

5. Season the sauce with the Worcestershire sauce and seasoned salt, then add the chicken meat, carrots, celery, cooked mushrooms, and pimientos. Stir well and continue heating just long enough to heat the chicken meat through. Serve hot with rice. If you plan to serve later it is wise to reheat in a double boiler over simmering water rather than over a direct flame.

CHICKEN MEXICAN STYLE

8 tablespoons (¼-pound stick) butter
2 3- to 4-pound fryers cut into serving pieces
2 1-pound cans stewed tomatoes, with their liquid
2 cloves garlic, peeled and crushed through a press
½ cup minced pimientos
2 teaspoons salt
2 tablespoons hot chili powder

1. Melt the butter in a large skillet and brown the chicken pieces in the butter on both sides.

2. Add the stewed tomatoes, garlic, pimientos, and salt; stir, bring to a simmer, cover the skillet, and cook the chicken over medium-low heat for about 20 minutes.

3. Stir in the chili powder and continue cooking another 10 minutes, covered.

4. Keep warm until serving time.

CHICKEN OR TURKEY POT PIE

1 cup flour
2 teaspoons double-acting baking powder
½ teaspoon salt
1½ tablespoons vegetable shortening
½ cup milk
5 tablespoons butter
6 tablespoons flour
1 teaspoon seasoned salt
½ teaspoon freshly ground white pepper
1 tablespoon Worcestershire sauce
2 tablespoons sherry
3 cups chicken broth *or* chicken consommé
4 cups cooked chicken or turkey meat, free of skin and bones and cut into bite-size pieces
1 cup cooked chopped carrots
1 cup cooked whole small mushrooms
1 cup cooked whole small onions

1. Sift the cup of flour with the baking powder and salt into a bowl. Cut the shortening into the flour and blend by hand. Add milk, gather dough into a mass, and knead just enough to make a smooth dough. Roll out into a circle the size of the top of the casserole.

2. Preheat oven to 450 degrees.

3. In a deep casserole melt the butter and stir in the 6 table-spoons of flour, making a smooth paste. Cook 3 minutes. Stir in the salt, pepper, Worcestershire sauce, and sherry. Then add the chicken broth a little at a time, stirring constantly to form a smooth, fairly thick sauce.

4. Add the cooked chicken or turkey meat to the sauce, and the carrots, mushrooms, and onions. Keep warm.

5. Place the circle of dough on top of chicken in sauce, slash in two or three places, put in oven, and bake 20 minutes until crust is golden brown. Serve immediately, directly from the casserole.

ROAST YOUNG CHICKENS, NATURAL GRAVY

2 young fryers (3 to 3½ pounds each) with giblets
2 teaspoons salt
4 tablespoons butter, softened
2 teaspoons poultry seasoning
2 slices bacon, cut in half
1½ cups chicken broth *or* chicken consommé
½ cup dry white wine

1. Preheat oven to 350 degrees.

2. Wash and dry the chickens inside and out. Salt the cavities, 1 teaspoon each.

3. Butter the outer skins of the chickens (2 tablespoons each). Sprinkle them with poultry seasoning, and lay ½ slice of bacon over each side of the breasts. Truss the chickens, arrange them on a roasting rack, and place in a roasting pan (or two) in the preheated oven. Roast for about 1 hour and 20 minutes.

4. When chickens are in the oven, put the broth in a saucepan over a low flame, add giblets, and simmer very gently. The broth should be reduced by one-third in volume by the time the chickens are done.

5. After the first 30 minutes of roasting, baste chickens with their pan drippings every 10 or 15 minutes, keeping skin moist, especially the breasts. Remove bacon after 1 hour of roasting.

6. When the chickens are done (skin golden brown, juice runs clear when thick part of leg is pricked), transfer the chickens to carving board or serving platter.

7. Add the broth (discard giblets or chop up to add to gravy) and wine to the drippings in the roasting pan. Hold pan over medium flame, scrape coagulated juices, and bring to a boil. Boil down to two-thirds of beginning volume. Strain into gravy boat and serve. Chickens may be carved in the kitchen and served in portions or carved at the table.

CHICKEN SAUTÉED WITH HAM AND MUSHROOMS

2 3- to 4-pound fryers, cut into serving pieces
4 tablespoons butter
6 slices cooked ham, cut into julienne strips
12 medium to large fresh mushrooms, sliced thin
½ cup grated onion
1 tablespoon fresh chopped parsley
1 teaspoon ground thyme
½ teaspoon salt
¼ teaspoon freshly ground black pepper
¼ cup brandy *or* cognac
2½ cups chicken broth *or* chicken consommé
1 tablespoon flour

1. Wash and pat dry the chicken pieces. Brown them in 3 tablespoons of the butter in a deep skillet equipped with a cover.

2. When the chicken is browned, stir in the julienned ham, mushroom slices, onion, parsley, thyme, salt, and pepper. Pour in the brandy and light it with a match. When the flames die, add ½ cup chicken broth, cover, and simmer for a total of 1 hour over medium heat.

3. During cooking time, occasionally add a little more broth to prevent burning.

4. When done, remove pieces of chicken from the pan. Add remaining chicken broth and bring to a boil. Separately, melt remaining tablespoon of butter, add flour, stir into a smooth paste, and cook 2 minutes. Beat this paste into the sauce in the skillet and cook until sauce thickens.

5. Replace chicken pieces in sauce, baste, and serve hot.

SOUTHERN FRIED CHICKEN

3 young fryers, cut into parts
½ teaspoon salt
¼ teaspoon freshly ground black pepper
¼ teaspoon cayenne
1 small garlic clove, peeled and minced very fine
4 cups vegetable oil *or* vegetable shortening for frying
2 cups flour for dredging

1. Wash and pat dry the chicken parts. Sprinkle them on both sides with salt, pepper, and cayenne, then distribute the garlic evenly over one side. Let the seasoned chicken stand at room temperature for 1 hour before cooking.

2. Heat the shortening or oil in a deep fryer to 375 degrees. Heat oven to 225 degrees and place a serving platter lined with paper towels inside.

3. Dredge the chicken parts, not more than two or three at a time, in the flour to form a light, even coating. Fry the parts to a golden brown color (12 to 15 minutes) and remove them to the warm platter in the oven as they get done.

4. Allow the last pieces to drain on the paper towels, then remove, transfer to a clean platter, and serve.

COQ AU VIN

This is an ideal dish to prepare in that clay cooker you bought recently but haven't gotten around to trying out!

2 3- to 4-pound fryers, cut into serving pieces
½ cup flour
8 tablespoons (¼-pound stick) butter
½ cup brandy *or* cognac
1 cup julienne strips of smoked ham
12 small whole onions, peeled
12 whole medium to small fresh mushrooms
½ teaspoon dried thyme
1 bay leaf
2 tablespoons fresh chopped parsley
1 teaspoon salt
¼ teaspoon freshly ground black pepper
2 cups dry red wine (the best you can afford)

1. Preheat oven to 325 degrees.

2. Prepare lid of the clay cooker according to instructions. Usually this requires soaking the lid in cold water for 10 or 15 minutes.

3. Pat the chicken pieces dry and dust them with the flour. Melt the butter in a skillet, brown the chicken pieces on all sides in the butter, and transfer them to the clay cooker as they are done.

4. Warm the brandy for about 1 minute in a small saucepan over a low flame.

5. Add the ham, onions, mushrooms, thyme, bay leaf, parsley,

salt, and pepper, then pour over the brandy and light it with a match. When flames die, pour in the wine.

6. Cover the clay cooker tightly and place in preheated oven. Bake 2¾ hours.

7. Serve Coq au Vin directly from clay cooker, with rice or noodles.

BRAISED DUCK

2 4- to 5-pound ducklings, oven ready
2 teaspoons salt
4 tablespoons butter
1 large onion, peeled and sliced
2 large apples, peeled, cored, and cut into rough chunks
2 cups dry red wine
¼ cup fresh lemon juice
1 teaspoon sugar

1. Use a large enameled stockpot large enough to accommodate both ducks. Otherwise it will be necessary to use two pots and divide the ingredients in half for each.

2. Rub the ducks with salt, melt the butter in the stockpot, and brown the ducks on all sides, handling them with long tongs. After the first duck is browned, set it aside and do the other one, then set it aside as well.

3. Brown the sliced onion in the same pot, then add apple chunks, wine, and the two ducks. Cover tightly and cook over a low flame for 1½ hours. After the first 45 minutes mix the lemon juice and sugar with the liquid in the pot.

4. To check whether ducks are done, prick one in the thickest part of the leg with a sharp point and make sure the juice runs clear; if not, cook a little longer and test again. When they are done, remove them from the pot; strain and degrease the liquid and use it as a gravy to accompany the ducks.

ROAST DUCKLINGS

2 oven-ready ducklings (about 5 pounds each)
½ teaspoon salt
¼ teaspoon freshly ground black pepper
1 medium onion, peeled and cut in half
½ cup Madeira wine

1. Preheat oven to 450 degrees.

2. Clip the wings off the ducks with a pair of poultry shears, as close to the body as possible. Set aside necks and giblets together with wings (to be used for sauce).

3. Dry the ducks well, inside and out. Salt and pepper the cavities and place ½ onion in each. Sew up cavities and truss ducks. Prick ducks all over with sharp knife point, especially in the fattiest places.

4. Roast the ducks on a rack in a large roasting pan in the preheated oven for 1 hour and 40 minutes. After the first 15 minutes reduce heat to 375 degrees. During roasting, remove fat from pan with basting bulb occasionally and prick skin again to release as much fat as possible.

5. When ready, transfer ducks to a warm platter in the turned-off oven, pour off most of the fat from the roasting pan, pour in

the Madeira, and hold the pan over a burner, scraping down coagulated juices. Strain this gravy into a sauce boat if ducks are to be served as is, carving at the table. If orange sauce will be made, then add strained sauce to the orange sauce.

ORANGE SAUCE FOR ROAST DUCKLINGS

    necks, wings, and giblets of 2 ducklings
1 tablespoon vegetable shortening
½ cup chopped onion
½ cup diced carrots
½ cup chopped celery
2 cups condensed beef consommé
2 tablespoons granulated sugar
2 tablespoons red wine vinegar
    rinds of 3 large oranges, cut into julienne strips and blanched in
    boiling water for 2 minutes
½ cup fresh orange juice, strained
1 tablespoon arrowroot
¼ cup orange liqueur (Curaçao, Cointreau, etc.)
    strained sauce from step 5 of the Roast Ducklings recipe

1. While ducks are roasting, use a cleaver to cut the wings and necks into 1-inch pieces. Brown them on all sides in the shortening in a large skillet, together with the giblets but not including the livers.

2. Remove pieces of duck from the skillet and reserve. Add onions, carrots, and celery to the pan and cook them over medium heat, stirring until carrots have browned slightly. Turn off heat. Remove vegetables and set aside.

3. Pour off fat from the skillet. Add about ½ cup of the consommé to the skillet, bring to a boil, scrape down any brown particles from the duck pieces and the vegetables, then strain liquid into a clean, medium-size saucepan.

4. Add the browned wings, necks, giblets, and the vegetables to the saucepan, plus the remaining consommé, and bring to a simmer.

5. Separately, in a small enameled skillet or saucepan, melt the sugar in the vinegar and cook until a medium-brown color is achieved. Add this caramel substance to the simmering sauce by pouring into it some sauce, mixing to dissolve caramel, and pouring back. After 45 minutes of simmering sauce uncovered, strain to remove duck pieces and vegetables and return strained sauce to pan.

6. Add blanched orange rind, mix arrowroot with the orange juice to dissolve completely, add this mixture to the sauce, and stir well. Add liqueur and finally strained sauce from roasting pan.

7. Stir over medium heat until sauce thickens slightly. Serve with ducklings, which should be carved at the table.

ROAST GOOSE WITH APPLE STUFFING

6 apples, peeled, cored, and cut into chunks
6 tablespoons butter
4 cups cubed toasted white bread
    goose liver, liquefied in a blender or with chopper
¼ cup minced onion
¼ cup finely chopped celery
2 teaspoons salt
¼ teaspoon freshly ground black pepper
1 egg
1 oven-ready goose, about 12 pounds
½ cup dry red wine
½ cup chicken broth

1. Put the apple chunks into a heavy enameled saucepan, cover, and cook over medium heat for 10 minutes, tossing occasionally. When done, turn off heat.

2. Melt the butter in a separate large saucepan, add the toast cubes, liver, onion, celery, 1 teaspoon of the salt, and the pepper. Cook 5 minutes over medium heat, turning two or three times to heat through. Then add partially cooked apple chunks and the egg, toss to mix well, and remove from heat. Allow the stuffing to cool.

3. Preheat oven to 350 degrees.

4. Rub the goose with the remaining 1 teaspoon salt, sprinkling a little in the cavity.

5. Stuff and truss the goose.

6. Roast the goose on a rack in a roasting pan in the preheated oven for 3 hours. Using a bulb baster, remove fat from the pan as it accumulates, and prick the skin of the goose occasionally to encourage runoff of fat.

7. When the goose is ready, remove it from the pan to a carving platter, pour off most of the fat, add the wine and chicken broth to the pan, hold it over a burner of the stove, and bring the liquid to a boil, scraping down the coagulated drippings from the bird. Reduce liquid by one-third. Strain it into a sauce boat and serve as a gravy with the stuffed goose, which should be carved at the table.

ROCK CORNISH GAME HENS
EN CASSEROLE

I strongly recommend fresh hens for this recipe. If the frozen variety is unavoidable, allow enough time for them to thaw completely at room temperature before beginning.

6 Rock Cornish game hens
4 to 6 tablespoons butter
2 carrots
2 medium-size onions
3 cups chicken broth *or* chicken consommé
1 cup dry white wine
1 bay leaf
½ teaspoon ground thyme
1 stalk celery, chopped into several pieces
1 tablespoon arrowroot *or* cornstarch
1 teaspoon salt
¼ teaspoon freshly ground black pepper

1. Dry the hens with a towel. In a casserole deep enough and large enough to accommodate all the hens, melt the butter over medium heat. Handling the hens one at a time with a long pair of tongs, brown them on all sides in the casserole. Set each one aside after browning.

2. Cut the carrots and onions into medium-thick slices and sauté them in the casserole in the butter remaining, for 5 minutes, turning frequently.

3. Add 1 cup of chicken broth to the vegetables and bring to a simmer, scraping up any particles on the bottom from the browning of the hens. Reduce this liquid by one-half.

4. Preheat oven to 325 degrees.

5. Add the browned hens, the other 2 cups of broth, wine, bay leaf, thyme, and celery. Bring this liquid to a simmer, uncovered, basting the hens frequently with it.

6. Cover the casserole tightly, place it in the preheated oven, and bake 45 minutes more.

7. Remove casserole from oven, quickly transfer the hens to a warm platter, which should then be placed in the turned-off oven.

8. Strain the liquid from the casserole into a saucepan. Mix the arrowroot with a little of the liquid in a small bowl or measuring cup until all the powder has dissolved. Now add it to the sauce and bring to a simmer, season with salt and pepper, and stir with a wire whisk until sauce thickens.

9. Serve the hens hot with the sauce in a gravy boat.

BARBECUED SQUABS

The perfect way to barbecue squabs is to put them on a revolving spit over glowing coals and sit back to watch them, sipping a frosty drink. This recipe, a combination of roasting and broiling, is intended to reproduce as closely as possible the results of this idyllic scene, but without leaving the home kitchen.

½ cup soy sauce
½ cup red wine vinegar
½ cup olive oil

¼ cup dry red wine
1 clove garlic, peeled and crushed through a press
1 bay leaf
2 tablespoons chopped onion
¼ teaspoon freshly ground black pepper
6 squabs, cleaned and oven-ready
6 strips bacon, cut in half

1. In a shallow dish large enough to hold all the squabs, combine the soy sauce, vinegar, oil, wine, garlic, bay leaf, onion, and pepper.

2. Wipe the squabs dry and place them in this marinade, then baste them with it every 10 minutes for an hour, also turning them so that all surfaces are immersed about the same amount of time.

3. Preheat oven to 350 degrees, and also preheat oven broiler if it is operated by a different heating element from the oven.

4. When the squabs have been marinated, transfer them to a roasting pan, reserving the liquid. Place the half-strips of bacon over the breasts and roast the squabs 50 minutes in the preheated oven, basting occasionally with a little marinade combined with any pan drippings.

5. After 50 minutes, turn all the squabs onto the same side and slide them under the broiler in the lowest position (maximum distance from heat). Broil 3 to 5 minutes until skin on exposed side begins to brown and sizzle but not burn. Baste with the marinade and watch carefully. Turn the squabs to the opposite side and repeat the process. Finally turn breast side up, remove any bacon strips that have not fallen off, and brown, basting more generously. Most or all of the marinade should have been used up at this point.

6. Serve the squabs immediately, making sure you provide sharp knives at the table.

ROAST YOUNG TURKEY WITH STUFFING

If you like white meat, try to make sure you get a female turkey. I do not believe in the false promise of "self-basting" birds, usually sold frozen hard as a rock and requiring a whole day to thaw. Get a fresh-killed unfrozen turkey and baste it yourself.

STUFFING INGREDIENTS

¼ pound butter
1 cup chopped onion
1 cup thinly sliced celery
1 cup thinly sliced mushrooms
2 cups chicken broth *or* chicken consommé
4 cups cubed stale French *or* sour dough bread
2 tablespoons fresh chopped parsley
2 tablespoons Worcestershire sauce
½ teaspoon freshly ground black pepper
½ teaspoon seasoned salt
  turkey liver

TURKEY

1 12- to 14-pound hen turkey, cleaned and oven-ready, with
  giblets separate
6 tablespoons butter, softened
1 tablespoon poultry seasoning
4 strips bacon, *or* 2 ⅛-inch-thick pieces lard, 6 inches by 4
  inches
2 cups chicken broth *or* chicken consommé

1. To make the stuffing, melt the ¼ pound of butter in a large saucepan over low heat, not allowing the butter to brown. Add the onions, celery, and mushrooms and cook 5 minutes, keeping heat low.

2. Pour in 2 cups of chicken broth and heat until the mixture is just barely simmering at the edges. Add bread cubes all at once, turn off heat and toss with 2 spoons to mix thoroughly with simmered vegetables. Add parsley, Worcestershire, pepper, and salt and toss again.

3. Liquefy the liver, using either a blender or a chopper. Add this to the stuffing and stir well. Set stuffing aside to insert just before roasting. The uncooked turkey should not be left stuffed for more than a few minutes.

4. Preheat oven to 425 degrees.

5. Stuff the cavity of the turkey with the stuffing, then secure with trussing needles and string. Butter the skin of the turkey all

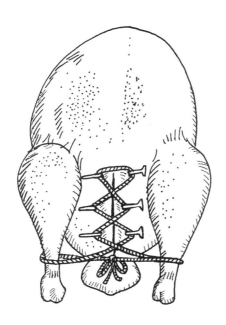

over with the softened butter, sprinkle on the poultry seasoning, place the bacon or lard so as to cover the breast, and place on a rack in a large roasting pan.

6. Roast the turkey for 15 minutes in the preheated oven, then reduce temperature setting to 325 degrees and roast 20 minutes per pound (4 to 5 hours depending on size). Using either a large spoon or a basting bulb, after the first hour of cooking time baste thoroughly every 15 minutes with the pan drippings, making sure to moisten entire bird, especially the breast.

7. When only about 30 minutes of cooking time are left, place the neck and giblets in a saucepan with 2 cups of chicken broth, bring to a simmer, and keep hot over a low flame.

8. When turkey is ready, carefully transfer it to a carving board or platter and discard lard or bacon pieces.

9. Pour off most of the fat from the roasting pan, discard neck and heart from the saucepan, and chop up the giblets very fine. Pour the broth in which the giblets were simmered into the roasting pan, along with chopped giblets. Holding the roasting pan over a burner on the stove (use two potholders), deglaze the pan by scraping up the brown drippings and bringing the broth to a boil. This step should be done very thoroughly both to extract maximum taste from the drippings and to save scrubbing time on the pan later!

10. Pour the gravy into a sauce boat and serve with the turkey. Carve at the table, spooning out portions of stuffing and gravy over all.

VI

Meats

ROAST PRIME RIBS OF BEEF
WITH YORKSHIRE PUDDING

This classic dish presents a slight problem in that two ovens are very convenient if you want the roast and the Yorkshire to be ready at the same time. However, it is recommended in many quarters to let a roast beef stand for some minutes after cooking before carving. Therefore, do not feel that a one-oven kitchen prevents you from serving Yorkshire pudding. One alternative is to make the pudding in a large toaster oven.

1 standing rib roast of beef, 3 ribs, about 7 pounds
1 teaspoon freshly ground black pepper
3 eggs
1½ cups milk
1½ cups flour, sifted
¾ teaspoon salt
6 tablespoons butter
½ cup beef broth *or* beef consommé
½ cup dry red wine

1. Preheat oven to 500 degrees.

2. Weigh the meat accurately. Calculate cooking time: 20 minutes per pound for rare, 24 minutes per pound for medium, or 28 minutes per pound for well done.

NOTE: I do not recommend roasting a good cut of beef to "well done." Even at "medium" there will be well-done pieces at the ends for those who insist on them.

3. Wipe the meat with a slightly dampened towel. Rub it all over with the pepper. Place in the roasting pan, bones down, fat

side up. Roast at the preheated temperature for 10 minutes, then reduce temperature setting to 350 degrees for remainder of the calculated roasting time.

4. About 30 minutes before the beef will be ready, combine the eggs, milk, flour, and salt in a mixing bowl and beat until the mixture is smooth. Melt the butter and pour it into a 9- by 12-inch ovenproof glass baking dish.

5. If you have a second oven, preheat it to 450 degrees. Place the dish of batter in the oven, and after 10 minutes reduce heat to 350 degrees. Continue baking 20 minutes more until the pudding has puffed up and is golden brown in color. If there is no second oven, then follow the same procedure immediately after removing the beef from the oven.

6. When the roast is ready, transfer it to a warm serving platter or carving board. Cover it with a towel.

7. Pour off most of the fat from the roasting pan, then add the beef broth and wine, hold the pan over a burner on the stove, bring the liquid to a simmer, and scrape down coagulated juices in the pan. Reduce liquid by one-third, then strain into a gravy boat.

8. Carve the roast at the table, cutting square pieces of Yorkshire to accompany, and pass around the gravy.

COLD ROAST FILLET OF BEEF

This dish is quite expensive and should be used for summer or buffet-style entertaining when there are other dishes being served as well, so that portions per person can be planned on the small side.

1 whole trimmed fillet of beef (about 5 to 6 pounds), tied, covered with thin slices of lard
½ cup Madeira wine
2 envelopes unflavored gelatin
3 cups beef consommé
4 sprigs fresh parsley

1. Preheat oven to 450 degrees.

2. Place tied fillet in a roasting pan and cook in preheated oven 10 minutes per pound (50 to 60 minutes). Remove meat from pan when done, remove strings and lard, and place on a platter. Refrigerate.

3. While meat is cooling, pour off most of the fat from the roasting pan, add the Madeira to the pan, and simmer it over a burner, scraping down coagulated juices. Strain into a medium-sized saucepan through a very fine mesh strainer or a piece of cheesecloth.

4. Dissolve the gelatin in 1 cup of the beef consommé. Then add gelatin mixture and remaining 2 cups of consommé to the strained Madeira. Bring to a simmer, stirring to make sure gelatin is completely melted and no grains are visible.

5. Pour the broth into a large jelly-roll pan (or two small ones) and refrigerate for several hours until jelled firm.

6. To serve, slice the fillet into ¼-inch slices and arrange on a decorative platter. With a small, sharp knife score the gelatin in the pans in parallel lines in both directions to form little squares or diamonds. Then remove gelatin cubes with a spatula and arrange them around the beef slices. Garnish platter with parsley sprigs and serve.

POT ROAST OF BEEF

1 large onion, peeled and sliced
1 bay leaf
2 teaspoons salt
½ teaspoon freshly ground black pepper
¼ teaspoon ground thyme
2 tablespoons white vinegar
3 tablespoons olive oil
3 cups dry red wine
1 4-pound pot roast, larded
1 clove garlic, peeled and crushed through a press
2 tablespoons brandy *or* cognac

1. Make a marinade consisting of the onion, bay leaf, salt, pepper, thyme, vinegar, oil, and wine.

2. Place the meat in a container just large enough to hold it with the liquids and marinate the meat overnight, turning at least three times during the period.

3. Preheat oven to 350 degrees.

4. Remove meat from marinade, reserving liquid.

5. Brown the meat on all sides in a hot skillet, handling meat with tongs to avoid piercing it. Set meat aside, pour marinade into skillet, and bring to a boil, scraping down meat particles in pan from browning process.

6. Put the meat in a deep casserole, pour over it the boiled marinade, add the crushed garlic and brandy, cover, and bake at least 3 hours until tender.

7. Transfer to warm platter and serve with the remaining liquid as gravy. If gravy looks too thin, reduce it by boiling down for a

few minutes. If not enough is left, add a little more red wine, heat to a simmer, then serve as before. The meat won't be harmed by waiting a few minutes for the gravy adjustments.

BLUE-CHEESE BURGERS

A pleasant change from the ordinary. Because blue cheese has a tangy, salty taste, there is no salt in this recipe.

1½ pounds freshly ground beef
3 tablespoons finely minced onion
1 egg
¼ teaspoon freshly ground black pepper
¼ pound blue cheese *or* Roquefort cheese
2 tablespoons sour cream
¼ cup flour
4 tablespoons vegetable oil *or* shortening for frying
6 hamburger buns (optional)

1. Combine the ground beef, onion, egg, and pepper in a bowl and blend well, using your hands.

2. In another bowl mash the blue cheese with the sour cream, using a fork, to produce a very thick paste. This step may be done with an electric mixer, but I advise using a deep bowl to avoid splattering. You may also use a blender, but be careful not to let the mixture liquefy.

3. Form the meat mixture into six equal-size patties about ¾ inch to 1 inch thick. Dust them with the flour and place them handy to the cooking surface.

4. Heat the oil or shortening on a griddle or skillet, then fry the patties on the first side for about 3 minutes (for medium rare). A longer time is needed for less rareness.

5. Turn the patties, and immediately, while they are cooking, spread a rounded tablespoon of the blue-cheese mixture on the top (cooked) side.

6. Fry 3 more minutes, then transfer immediately to plates or onto hamburger buns and serve. The buns may be toasted if desired.

MINUTE STEAKS WITH HERB BUTTER

8 tablespoons (¼-pound stick) butter
1 tablespoon finely minced fresh parsley
½ teaspoon dried tarragon
1 tablespoon fresh chopped chives
6 boned, ½-inch-thick sirloin steaks, pounded to ¼-inch thickness
2 tablespoons olive oil
½ teaspoon freshly ground black pepper

1. Soften the butter at room temperature until very soft but not melted. In a mixing bowl combine the butter with parsley, tarragon, and chives. Mix very thoroughly with a fork to distribute herbs evenly. Chill in refrigerator.

2. Heat a skillet over medium flame until it is very hot. Rub the steaks with olive oil and pepper on both sides. Fry in the skillet about 60 seconds on each side for medium rare.

3. Serve steaks immediately with a rounded tablespoon of the herb butter on each, just melting from the heat of the meat when served.

SLICED BEEF IN TOMATO SAUCE

3 cups beef broth *or* beef consommé
2 stalks celery, chopped
2 carrots, cut in half lengthwise
1 large onion, peeled and quartered
½ teaspoon ground thyme
¼ teaspoon freshly ground black pepper
1 3½- to 4-pound piece of brisket *or* eye of round
4 tablespoons butter
8 tomatoes, sliced thin
1 tablespoon flour
3 egg yolks

1. Bring the beef broth to a boil with 2½ quarts of water in a stockpot or large saucepan. Add the celery, carrots, onion, thyme, and pepper, then place the meat in the broth.

2. Cover partially and cook at a slow simmer for 2½ hours.

3. When done, remove meat and set aside. Strain broth into another container and save the pieces of carrot and celery.

4. Preheat oven to 350 degrees.

5. Melt 2 tablespoons of the butter in a medium-size saucepan, add the reserved pieces of cooked vegetables, and cook for 2 minutes, stirring.

6. Add the sliced tomatoes and ½ cup of the reserved broth and simmer 20 minutes. Run the contents of the saucepan through a strainer to remove seeds.

7. Melt the remaining 2 tablespoons of butter, stir in the flour, and stir into a smooth paste, cooking 3 minutes. Stir the strained tomato sauce into this paste and add a little more broth if needed. Simmer the sauce until it thickens. When the sauce achieves the desired consistency (a fairly thick gravy), remove from heat.

8. Using a wire whisk and beating constantly off heat, beat the egg yolks into the sauce, one at a time, until all three are incorporated.

9. With a very sharp slicing knife, cut the meat into thin slices. Arrange the slices, overlapping a little, in an ovenproof baking dish. Ladle the sauce over them and bake 25 minutes in the preheated oven. Serve hot.

BOILED BEEF TONGUE

1 fresh beef tongue (3 to 3½ pounds)
1 large carrot, peeled and cut in half lengthwise
1 large onion, peeled and quartered
2 stalks celery, chopped
5 peppercorns, cracked
1 bay leaf
3 tablespoons butter
3 tablespoons flour
1 cup beef broth *or* beef consommé
1 cup dry red wine

1. Wash and dry the tongue. Place it with the carrot, onion, celery, peppercorns, and bay leaf in enough water to cover it by 2 inches in a stockpot. Bring to a boil and reduce heat to a simmer.

2. After cooking about 2 hours, remove tongue from the pot with tongs, remove the skin, which should now be quite easy to peel off, and return the tongue to the pot for 1 more hour.

3. When tongue is done, remove it to a warm platter.

4. Melt the butter in a saucepan and stir in the flour. Stir to a smooth paste and cook 3 minutes.

5. Add the beef broth a little at a time, then the wine in the same manner, stirring all the while. Take the vegetables from the cooking liquid and rub them through a sieve into the sauce. Bring the sauce to a simmer, and if it is too thick, dilute with a little of the cooking liquid from the tongue, but do not add the bay leaf or peppercorns.

6. To serve, slice the tongue into thin slices, pour on the hot gravy, and serve.

GRILLED LOIN LAMB CHOPS

These may be cooked in the oven broiler, but I strongly recommend using a stove-top grill with raised ridges and a corner well, which fits over two burners.

12 trimmed, 1-inch-thick loin lamb chops
1 tablespoon medium to strong mustard
½ teaspoon freshly ground black pepper
6 sprigs parsley

1. Heat grill (or preheat oven broiler) until very hot. Reduce heat to medium.

2. Rub the chops on both sides with mustard and then sprinkle them with pepper.

3. Grill or broil chops 6 to 8 minutes on each side.

4. Serve immediately, garnished with parsley sprigs.

ROAST LEG OF LAMB

1 leg of lamb, 6 to 8 pounds
2 garlic cloves
1 tablespoon hot English mustard
½ teaspoon freshly ground black pepper
½ cup dry red wine
½ cup beef broth *or* beef consommé

1. Preheat oven to 350 degrees.

2. Wipe leg of lamb with a damp cloth, then weigh it accurately.

3. Peel the garlic cloves and cut them into thin slivers. Using a small, sharp paring knife, cut slits in the meat and slip the slivers of garlic into the slits. Try to distribute them as evenly as possible around the surface of the meat. Rub the meat with the mustard and sprinkle it with the pepper.

4. Calculate the roasting time at 20 minutes to the pound, and roast the leg on a rack in the roasting pan, fat side up, for the prescribed time. No basting is required.

5. When meat is ready, remove the leg and the rack from the roasting pan, setting the meat on a warm platter or a carving board. Let it stand while you prepare the gravy.

6. Pour most of the fat out of the roasting pan, then add the wine and beef broth to it. Hold the pan over a burner on top of the stove, bring the liquid to a boil, and scrape down all the drippings to deglaze the pan. Simmer to reduce the volume of liquid by about one-third. Pour hot gravy into a sauce boat and bring to the table.

7. Carve the lamb by cutting thin slices with a very sharp knife. The meat should be slightly pink toward the center, closest to the bone.

SHASHLIK OF LAMB

This dish requires long (10- to 12-inch) skewers, which can be metal or wood, and may be prepared on a stove-top grill, on an outdoor barbecue, or in an oven broiler. Have the butcher cut up a leg of lamb into 1-inch cubes, allowing about five cubes per person for a generous portion.

4 to 5 pounds cubed leg of lamb
1 cup soy sauce
1 cup red wine vinegar
1 tablespoon sugar
1 tablespoon dried garlic chips
¼ teaspoon freshly ground black pepper
½ cup olive oil
2 tablespoons lemon juice
6 medium to small onions

6 strips bacon
24 medium-size mushrooms
4 tablespoons butter
½ cup dry white wine

1. Wash the meat cubes under cold running water and pat them dry with paper towels.

2. Combine the soy sauce, vinegar, sugar, garlic, pepper, oil, and lemon juice in a large rectangular Pyrex dish, add the meat, baste, and refrigerate. Allow the meat to marinate for at least 1 hour, and as long as 4 hours. Turn the meat in the marinade occasionally.

3. While the meat is marinating, bring about 3 quarts of water to a boil in a large saucepan and immerse the onions in it for about 3 minutes, then remove them. Blanch the bacon strips in the same boiling water for 2 minutes, and remove them with a slotted spoon. Cut the bacon strips into 4 pieces each, and peel and quarter the onions.

4. Remove the stems from the mushrooms with a gentle twist, then clean the caps carefully with a damp cloth. Melt the butter in a large skillet equipped with a cover, add the mushroom caps and the white wine, cover, and cook over low heat for 20 minutes, turning the caps once. Remove the caps from the skillet and set aside, but reserve the cooking liquid.

5. Heat oven broiler or stove-top grill. While it is heating, arrange the food on each of six skewers as follows: one lamb cube, one mushroom cap, one square of bacon, one onion quarter; repeat until you end up with the fifth lamb cube at the other end. Pour the mushroom cooking liquid into the marinade and hold ready near broiler.

6. Broil the skewers 4 minutes on each of the four sides, basting repeatedly with the liquid to keep moist, making sure to moisten the mushrooms and onions as well as the meat.

7. I recommend serving the shashlik with rice and using any remaining marinade as extra sauce, heating it quickly before serving.

IRISH LAMB STEW

3 pounds leg of lamb meat, cut into 1-inch cubes
4 large potatoes, peeled and cut into ½-inch slices
2 large onions, peeled and sliced thin
2 stalks celery, washed and chopped
¾ teaspoon dried thyme
1 bay leaf
2 tablespoons fresh chopped parsley
2 teaspoons salt
½ teaspoon freshly ground black pepper

1. Preheat oven to 350 degrees.

2. Heat a large cast-iron skillet over medium heat, then brown the lamb cubes on all sides, turning frequently and doing only a few at a time to prevent burning. Remove browned cubes from the skillet as they are done and place them in a deep casserole equipped with a cover.

3. To the meat in the casserole add all the remaining ingredients. Using two large spoons, turn and mix so that the meat is dispersed throughout.

4. Cover stew ingredients by ½ inch with cold water, cover pot, place in preheated oven, and bake at least 2 hours, until meat is tender and potatoes are cooked through.

NOTE: This stew is very good reheated.

BAKED PORK CHOPS

6 pork loin chops, 1 inch to 1¼ inches thick
¼ teaspoon freshly ground black pepper
1 medium onion, peeled and sliced very thin
3 large tomatoes, peeled and seeded
½ cup beef broth *or* beef consommé
1 tablespoon soy sauce

1. Preheat oven to 375 degrees.

2. Heat a large ovenproof skillet equipped with a cover over medium heat. Rub the pork chops on both sides with the pepper, then brown them on both sides in the skillet, about 2 minutes on each side.

3. Remove the browned chops from the skillet and set them aside. Put the sliced onion in the skillet, sauté until slightly colored, then add the tomato pulp and stir over medium heat for 1 minute. Turn off heat, replace pork chops in the skillet, and pour in beef broth and soy sauce. Stir, baste, cover skillet, and place in preheated oven.

4. Bake chops 1 hour, uncovering for the last 10 minutes.

5. To serve, transfer baked chops to a warm platter, pass remaining onions, tomato, and liquid from pan through a strainer, and spoon resulting sauce over the chops.

ROAST LOIN OF PORK WITH APPLES

This slightly unorthodox method of cooking the apples with the meat results in a savory, moist accompaniment that precludes the need for a separate gravy.

1 5- to 6-pound center-cut pork loin roast
1 teaspoon salt
¼ teaspoon freshly ground black pepper
¼ teaspoon ground thyme
4 pounds cooking apples
2 tablespoons sugar
1 teaspoon ground cinnamon

1. Preheat oven to 350 degrees.

2. Weigh meat accurately and calculate roasting time at 30 minutes per pound.

3. Mix the salt, pepper, and thyme together in a small bowl and sprinkle over the meat.

4. Place the meat, bones down and fat side up, in a large roasting pan, allowing plenty of room on all sides for the apples. Place in the oven and note the time.

5. While meat is roasting, peel, quarter, and core the apples, then cut the quarters into ½-inch chunks. Put the apple chunks in a heavy enamel saucepan, sprinkle with a mixture of the sugar and cinnamon, cover, and cook over medium heat for about 15 minutes, stirring occasionally, until apples have softened slightly and the liquid has begun to boil.

6. Turn off heat under apples. When there is 1 hour left of the roasting time for the meat, remove as much of the fat as possible

from the roasting pan with a bulb baster. Spoon partially cooked apples into roasting pan around the meat and return to the oven for the last hour.

7. When serving, carve loin chops and spoon hot apples over each serving.

FRESH HAM POT ROAST

2 tablespoons olive oil
1 3- to 4-pound fresh ham
¾ cup chopped onion
2 large carrots, peeled and chopped
1 turnip, peeled and diced
2 stalks celery, chopped
2 tablespoons chopped parsley
3 fresh tomatoes, diced
2 cups beef broth *or* beef consommé
1 teaspoon Maggi liquid seasoning

1. Preheat oven to 375 degrees.

2. Using a heavy enameled saucepan or stockpot equipped with a cover, heat the olive oil, then brown the fresh ham on all sides in the hot oil.

3. Reduce heat and add the onion, carrots, turnip, celery, parsley, tomatoes, and 1 cup of the beef broth to the meat in the pot.

4. Cover the pot, place in the preheated oven, and bake at least 2½ hours, until the ham is cooked through.

5. When ready, remove meat to a warm platter, add the second cup of beef broth and the Maggi to the pot, and bring to a boil, scraping down vegetables and any meat drippings inside the pot.

6. Reduce sauce by about one-third by boiling, then skim most of the fat from the surface and transfer liquid to a gravy boat.

7. To serve, slice the fresh ham into thin slices and pour hot gravy over.

BARBECUED SPARE RIBS
CHINESE STYLE

Hoisin sauce, which gives the ribs in this recipe their characteristic flavor, is available canned in oriental food shops, many gourmet food shops or departments, and sometimes in ordinary supermarkets.

½ cup hoisin sauce
¼ cup soy sauce
3 tablespoons tomato catsup
3 tablespoons granulated sugar
3 tablespoons sherry
½ teaspoon garlic powder
2 whole racks spareribs (total, about 5 to 6 pounds)
1 cup Chinese plum sauce
¼ cup hot mustard

1. In a large shallow dish, combine the hoisin, soy sauce, catsup, sugar, sherry, and garlic powder and mix well.

2. Cut partially through the meat between the ribs. Rub the racks of ribs with the marinade on both sides, then let them stand in the remaining marinade for 2 hours, turning occasionally.

3. Preheat oven to 350 degrees.

4. Place two roasting pans filled with hot water about 1½ inches deep side by side in the preheated oven. Place the ribs on metal racks over the hot water. Reserve any marinade remaining for basting. The steam from the pans of hot water rises and envelops ribs during cooking, preventing the sugar in the marinade from burning black.

5. Roast the ribs 1½ hours, basting occasionally and turning the ribs over every 20 minutes. For the last 10 minutes raise the temperature to 450 degrees.

6. To serve, remove from oven and cut through between the bones to separate ribs. They may be served with Chinese plum sauce (also available in cans) and hot mustard if desired.

BAKED VEAL CHOPS
WITH MUSHROOMS

6 1-inch-thick large veal chops
6 tablespoons butter
1 cup dry white wine
1 cup chicken broth *or* chicken consommé
1 stalk celery, chopped
1 bay leaf
2 tablespoons chopped parsley
½ teaspoon salt
¼ teaspoon freshly ground black pepper
1 pound fresh white mushrooms, cut in half

1. In an ovenproof skillet equipped with a cover, brown the chops on both sides in the butter over medium heat. Remove the chops and pour off butter and fat.

2. Preheat oven to 325 degrees.

3. Add the wine, chicken broth, celery, bay leaf, parsley, salt, pepper, and mushrooms to the skillet, bring to a simmer, and put back the browned chops.

4. Simmer until the liquid is reduced by one-third and slightly thickened.

5. Cover the skillet and bake in preheated oven 45 minutes.

6. Remove from oven and serve chops, spooning some sauce with mushrooms over each portion.

ROAST LEG OF VEAL

A leg of veal roast tastes much better with the bone left in than boned. It is handled very much like a leg of lamb, except for the covering of lard to maintain moistness.

1 whole leg of veal, trimmed (about 5 to 6 pounds)
¼ teaspoon salt
¼ teaspoon freshly ground black pepper
4 thin pieces lard *or* salt pork, 3 inches by 2 inches
½ cup beef broth *or* beef consommé
¼ cup light dry red *or* rosé wine
2 tablespoons butter, softened

1. Preheat oven to 375 degrees. Weigh the meat accurately and calculate cooking time at 20 minutes per pound.

2. Wipe the veal and rub all over with a mixture of the salt and pepper combined. Tie the lard onto the meat so that one of the two flat surfaces is covered. Place on a rack in a roasting pan lard side up and roast in the preheated oven for the calculated cooking time. Basting is not necessary.

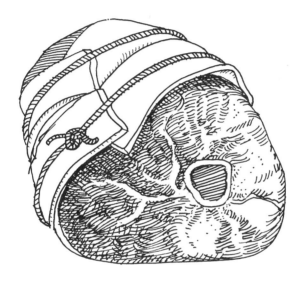

3. For the final 15 minutes of roasting time cut through the strings and remove the lard.

4. When done, place the meat on a platter in the turned-off oven.

5. Pour off as much of the fat from the roasting pan as possible. Add beef broth and wine to the pan, hold it over a burner on top of the stove, and bring the liquid to a boil, scraping down coagulated juices. Strain gravy into a sauce boat and swirl in the softened butter enrichment just before serving. Carve the roast at the table.

PICCATA OF VEAL

12 thin slices of veal (from the leg)
¼ teaspoon salt
⅛ teaspoon freshly ground black pepper
4 tablespoons flour
2 tablespoons olive oil
3 tablespoons butter
¼ cup chicken broth
2 tablespoons lemon juice
4 tablespoons minced fresh parsley

1. Pound the veal slices flat between two sheets of waxed paper with the side of a cleaver or with a flat meat mallet.

2. Place a platter in a warm (250-degree) oven.

3. Mix the salt, pepper, and flour together, then dredge the veal slices in this mixture so that a very thin coating adheres to both sides.

4. Heat the oil and butter together in a large skillet. Fry the veal slices in the skillet over high heat about 30 to 40 seconds, until golden. Cook only three or four slices at a time. Transfer each batch to the warm platter before starting the next.

5. Pour off all but 1 tablespoon of the fat from the skillet, then add the chicken broth and lemon juice and bring to a boil, scraping down any particles from cooking the veal.

6. Reduce liquid by about one-third, then pour it over the veal slices in the platter, sprinkle on parsley, and serve.

SCALOPPINE OF VEAL MARSALA

12 thin slices of veal (from the leg)
1 cup milk
1 egg
2 cups thinly sliced mushrooms
3 tablespoons butter
¾ cup Marsala wine
2 tablespoons fresh chopped parsley
¼ teaspoon freshly ground black pepper
¼ teaspoon salt
¾ cup fine white bread crumbs *or* matzo meal
3 tablespoons olive oil

1. Pound the veal slices flat between two pieces of waxed paper with the flat side of a cleaver or a flat meat mallet.

2. In a shallow dish beat the milk and egg together; put in the pounded cutlets to soak for 1 hour.

3. After soaking time, sauté the sliced mushrooms in the butter over low heat until they are softened but not browned. Add the wine, parsley, and salt and pepper to the pan, cover, and simmer over low heat while you prepare the veal in a separate skillet.

4. Heat a large skillet over medium heat. Remove the veal cutlets from the milk mixture and coat them on both sides with the bread crumbs. Add the olive oil to the skillet and when it starts to sizzle, fry the coated cutlets about 1 minute on each side until golden brown.

5. Set the cooked cutlets on paper towels for a few seconds on each side to drain and place them on a warm platter.

6. Spoon the mushrooms and Marsala sauce from the other pan over the veal and serve hot.

MEAT LOAF

2 pounds lean ground round steak
¾ pound ground pork shoulder
2 slices bacon, cut into ¼-inch strips
1 clove garlic, peeled and crushed through a press
3 tablespoons finely chopped parsley
¼ cup beef broth
1 cup cubed white bread (¼-inch cubes)
2 eggs
2 tablespoons brandy *or* cognac
1 teaspoon salt
¼ teaspoon freshly ground black pepper
½ teaspoon ground thyme
¼ teaspoon dried rosemary
4 slices bacon

1. Mix together in a large bowl the meats, ¼-inch bacon strips, garlic, and parsley.

2. Pour the beef broth over the bread cubes and add them to the meat, kneading by hand to mix well. Be careful not to over-mix the meat, though, as it will turn "tough."

3. Beat the eggs, stir into them the brandy, salt, pepper, thyme, and rosemary. Add this liquid to the meat and work it into the mixture thoroughly by hand.

4. Preheat oven to 350 degrees.

5. Pack the meat mixture into a standard 9-by-5-by-3-inch loaf pan and cover top with the 4 slices of bacon laid out lengthwise. Bake in the preheated oven 1 hour and 20 minutes.

6. To unmold, pass a sharp knife around the edges of the loaf pan. Remove bacon slices and discard. Reverse the loaf onto a warm serving platter and serve. There will be plenty of juice, which should be spooned from the platter onto each serving.

VII

Vegetables and Salads

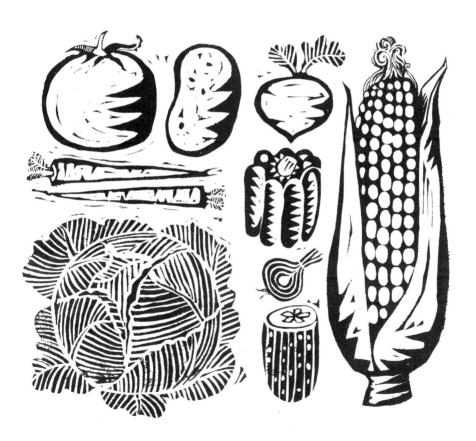

ARTICHOKES VINAIGRETTE

6 medium to large artichokes
1 lemon
3 tablespoons olive oil
1 clove garlic, peeled and cut in half
10 peppercorns, cracked
1 tablespoon white vinegar

1. With a pair of kitchen shears, trim the sharp points from the leaves of the artichokes. With a heavy chef's knife or cleaver, cut

½ inch from the tops of the artichokes, and trim the bottoms so that they will sit level.

2. Cut the lemon in half, and squeezing slightly as you work, rub all the cut surfaces with the flesh of the lemon.

3. To about 2 inches of water in a large saucepan or stockpot add the oil, garlic, peppercorns, and vinegar. Set a steamer platform in the water and place the artichokes on the platform. If necessary use two pots, or do the steaming in two shifts. Cover and steam 45 minutes, adding a little water if necessary.

4. When done, remove the artichokes from the pot and cool them to room temperature, then refrigerate the cooked artichokes until ready to serve.

VINAIGRETTE SAUCE

Almost any variety of oil-and-vinegar-based dressing is acceptable to serve with the artichokes.

¾ cup olive oil
¼ cup red wine vinegar
½ teaspoon salt
¼ teaspoon freshly ground black pepper
1 tablespoon finely chopped chives
1 tablespoon chopped parsley
1 hard-cooked egg, rubbed through a sieve

Combine all the ingredients in a bowl and mix well. Serve in individual small cups with the artichokes, or in the sauce basin of special artichoke serving plates if available.

FRESH STEAMED ASPARAGUS
WITH HOLLANDAISE SAUCE

The best way to cook asparagus, whether you intend to eat it hot or cold, is to steam it standing up in a tall pot, covered. This is better than cooking it with the spears lying down because the tougher, thicker ends are closer to the heat source and thus cook more in the same time, while the tips, which are more delicate and require less cooking, are protected by their distance from the heat from overcooking.

1 large bunch fresh asparagus (at least 6 pieces per person)
4 egg yolks
2 teaspoons lemon juice
12 tablespoons (1½ sticks) butter
¼ teaspoon salt

1. Wash the asparagus, then arrange it in a bundle, lining up the tips evenly and letting the thick ends be uneven. Tie the bundle tight with white string, making two separate ties to hold it together securely. Take a large, sharp chef's knife or cleaver and cut off the thick ends evenly in one stroke, removing about ½ inch from the shortest one. The result should be that all the asparagus spears are of identical length. Stand the bunch up in a tall pot, add 2 inches of water, cover, and steam 20 minutes.

2. Make the Hollandaise Sauce while the asparagus is cooking. Over simmering but not boiling water in a double boiler, with a wire whisk beat the egg yolks and lemon juice with one-third of the butter (4 tablespoons) until the butter is melted. Continue beating and add another 4 tablespoons of butter, and when it has been absorbed do the same for the last 4 tablespoons. Continue

beating until the sauce has thickened, then off heat stir in the salt with a few strokes.

3. When the asparagus is cooked, remove the whole bunch from the pot with a large pair of tongs, cut the string, lay the bunch on its side in a serving dish in which you have placed a cloth napkin to absorb excess moisture, and bring to the table.

4. Serve the asparagus on separate plates, spooning the Hollandaise Sauce over the asparagus generously.

PUREE OF FRESH BEETS

This recipe will turn the most obdurate beet hater into a beet lover! I especially recommend serving this dish with lamb.

5 to 6 pounds fresh beets
4 tablespoons butter
3 tablespoons flour
1 cup beef broth *or* beef consommé
1 tablespoon lemon juice
2 to 3 tablespoons sugar
2 teaspoons Maggi liquid seasoning *or* Worcestershire sauce *or* soy sauce

1. Scrub the beets under cold running water and trim off roots and stalks, but do not peel. Place them on a steamer platform in a large pot over boiling water and steam them, covered, for about 45 minutes or until tender. To test, insert a sharp knife into the flesh of a beet. It should slide in without much resis-

tance. Check occasionally during the steaming and add water to the pot if it has boiled down too low.

2. When done, remove the beets from the steamer, reserving the liquid. Allow them to cool. Strain the liquid through two thicknesses of cheesecloth wrung out in cold water and hold ready near the stove. When the beets are cool enough to handle, peel off outer skin; it should slip off quite easily. Grate the peeled beets through the coarse blade of a grater or use an electric food processor. Pour off excess liquid from the grated beets into the other beet liquid by the stove.

3. Over simmering water in a large double boiler, melt the butter, add the flour, stir into a paste, and cook 3 minutes. Now add the beef broth little by little, followed by enough of the beet liquid to produce a medium-thick texture. Add the lemon juice, sugar, and seasoning.

4. Add the grated beets to the sauce, stir well, and heat in the double boiler for about 15 to 20 minutes until hot throughout.

NOTE: Leftovers may be reheated or frozen for future use.

BROCCOLI SOUFFLÉ

1 tablespoon butter, softened
½ cup fine dry white bread crumbs
1½ pounds fresh broccoli
¼ pound butter
½ cup all-purpose flour
2½ cups heavy cream
3 eggs, separated
2 tablespoons Worcestershire sauce
½ teaspoon seasoned salt
¼ teaspoon freshly ground black pepper

1. Preheat oven to 350 degrees.

2. Grease an 8-cup soufflé dish or ring mold with the softened butter and dust inside surfaces with the bread crumbs so that they adhere.

3. Wash and steam the broccoli on a steamer platform over boiling water in a deep, covered saucepan for 20 minutes or until tender. After cooling the broccoli to room temperature, chop the cooked broccoli very fine.

4. Melt the ¼ pound butter in a saucepan. Add flour, stir into a smooth paste, then add heavy cream a little at a time, stirring to make a smooth, thick white sauce.

5. Beat the egg yolks separately, then off heat stir them into the white sauce along with the Worcestershire sauce, salt, and pepper.

6. Beat the egg whites in a mixing bowl until they form stiff peaks.

7. Combine the white sauce with the chopped broccoli, then fold the beaten egg whites into this mixture very gently.

8. Pour the batter into the buttered soufflé dish or mold and bake in the preheated oven about 30 minutes until the soufflé has puffed up. Serve hot, directly from the soufflé dish, or reverse mold onto a serving platter first.

NOTE: If you use a metal ring mold, cooking time should be a few minutes less. To unmold, pass a sharp knife all around edges, then reverse onto platter, tapping bottom of mold with a wooden spoon to dislodge.

FRESH CREAMED CORN
OFF THE COB

Many people serve corn only at the most informal meals simply because handling corn on the cob at the table is considered messy. This recipe provides the same delicious fresh taste in a form more amenable to elegant dining.

10 to 12 ears fresh corn
4 tablespoons butter
2 tablespoons flour
1 cup heavy cream
1 teaspoon seasoned salt
1 teaspoon Worcestershire sauce

1. Remove the husks and silk from the ears of corn. With a small, sharp paring knife cut the kernels away from the cobs into a bowl.

2. Melt the butter in a saucepan large enough to hold all the corn easily, stir the flour into it, and cook the paste for 3 minutes, stirring and not allowing it to brown. Add the cream a little at a time until a smooth sauce is formed. If at this point the sauce is very thick, dilute it with a little water or with the juice that has collected at the bottom of the bowl of corn kernels.

3. Add the kernels to the sauce, stir in the salt and Worcestershire sauce, and cook over low heat until heated through. Cover and keep warm until serving time, and make sure to serve additional salt and pepper at the table for those who prefer stronger seasoning.

STUFFED BAKED POTATOES

6 large baking potatoes
1 dozen slices bacon
¾ cup thinly sliced scallions, including the green ends
1½ cups sour cream
½ cup grated Swiss *or* Romano cheese
1 teaspoon salt
½ teaspoon freshly ground black pepper
2 tablespoons chopped parsley

1. Preheat oven to 400 degrees.

2. Scrub the potato skins and bake the potatoes in the preheated oven for 1 hour. Do *not* wrap in foil.

3. Remove potatoes from oven and allow them to cool slightly while preparing stuffing.

4. Fry the bacon in a large skillet until crisp. Drain on paper towels, then crumble bacon and set aside. Pour off half the bacon fat from the skillet.

5. Add the scallions to the skillet, sauté them 2 or 3 minutes in the bacon fat. Off heat, stir in sour cream and grated cheese.

6. Cut potatoes open with one cut lengthwise across tops, carefully scoop out most of the potato flesh with a teaspoon, and add flesh to skillet. Blend with a potato masher in the skillet with cream and cheese mixture.

7. Stir in salt, pepper, and crumbled bacon, then stuff the potato shells with the mixture, piling it high above the level of the skin.

8. Bake the potatoes again for 15 minutes, sprinkle with chopped parsley, and serve hot.

FRENCH-FRIED POTATOES

4 to 6 mature potatoes, even-shaped and oblong, if possible
4 to 6 cups vegetable oil *or* shortening for deep frying
  salt

1. Peel the potatoes and cut them into thin, long pieces, not more than ¼ inch by ¼ inch by the length of the potato. Lay out on paper towels to remove all surface moisture.

2. Bring oil in deep fryer to a temperature of 475 degrees. Use a fat thermometer if the fryer has no thermostat.

3. Lower a handful of potatoes in the wire basket into the oil and fry to a golden brown, shaking the basket occasionally to prevent sticking.

4. Drain finished potatoes on paper towels and keep warm in the oven at a low setting until all are done. Salt liberally and serve.

CHINESE FRIED RICE

⅓ cup peanut oil
¾ cup finely sliced scallions, including the green ends
½ cup diced cooked shrimp
½ cup diced cooked pork
½ cup diced cooked beef
¾ cup cooked (or canned) peas, drained
6 cups cooked rice
3 tablespoons soy sauce
1 teaspoon sugar
2 eggs, beaten

1. Heat the oil in a large skillet or deep saucepan or wok, without allowing it to smoke. Add the scallions and stir them in hot oil for 2 minutes. Then add shrimp, meats, and peas and stir 2 more minutes to heat.

2. Break up the cooked rice in a bowl if sticky, add it to the pan, toss well to coat with oil, and mix with vegetables and meats. Heat through, tossing frequently.

3. Stir in soy sauce and sugar and blend well.

4. At this point the fried rice can be kept hot on a warming tray until just before serving.

5. To serve, stir beaten eggs into the fried rice just long enough so that they cook from the heat and are well distributed but still fairly soft. Serve immediately.

SAFFRON RICE

A wonderful way to pep up rice for use with almost any meat dish.

4 tablespoons butter
½ cup finely chopped onion
1 garlic clove, peeled and crushed through a press
1 cup uncooked rice
2½ cups chicken broth
1 teaspoon salt
1 pinch saffron

1. Using a heavy enameled saucepan equipped with a cover, melt the butter over medium heat and sauté the chopped onion and crushed garlic for 2 or 3 minutes, until the onion is soft and transparent.

2. Add the rice, chicken broth, salt, and saffron and stir briskly.

3. Bring to a boil uncovered, then reduce heat to produce a simmer, cover, and cook 12 to 14 minutes, until all the liquid is absorbed. Do not let the rice burn on the bottom. Keep hot on warming tray until ready to serve.

CREAMED FRESH SPINACH

The main thing to remember about spinach is that what looks like a lot at the vegetable stand shrinks down to look like very little when it's cooked. So don't be alarmed by the quantity recommended.

1½ pounds fresh spinach leaves
4 tablespoons butter
2 tablespoons minced onion
3 tablespoons flour
½ teaspoon salt
¼ teaspoon freshly ground white pepper
¾ cup heavy cream

1. Wash the spinach in cold water to remove all dirt and sand. Cut away and discard thick stems.

2. Bring 1 quart of water to a boil in a large saucepan, add washed and trimmed leaves, and cook, covered, at a simmer for 20 minutes. Drain in a colander.

3. Chop the spinach fine with a chopper or chef's knife, or use an electric blender.

4. In a medium-size saucepan melt the butter, add the onion, and cook 2 or 3 minutes to soften but not brown over medium heat.

5. Stir in the flour to make a smooth paste, cook 3 minutes more, stirring.

6. Add the salt and pepper and the heavy cream a little at a time; continue cooking and stirring to make a smooth sauce. Do not boil.

7. Finally add the chopped spinach and stir over medium heat until hot and ready to serve.

SPINACH LIGHTLY SAUTÉED
IN GARLIC

1½ pounds fresh spinach leaves
1 tablespoon olive oil
2 cloves garlic, peeled and halved
4 tablespoons butter
1 tablespoon white vinegar
½ teaspoon salt
¼ teaspoon freshly ground black pepper

1. Follow steps 1 and 2 of the recipe for Creamed Fresh Spinach, page 169.

2. In a large skillet heat the olive oil over medium heat, add the garlic, and cook about 5 minutes, mashing garlic pieces down with the back of a wooden spoon.

3. Remove garlic fragments, add butter, and let it melt. Add hot drained cooked spinach to skillet. Using two slotted spoons, turn spinach to pick up garlic flavor from oil and butter and absorb them.

4. Sprinkle vinegar, salt, and pepper onto spinach, turn a few more times, and serve hot.

STEAMED STRING BEANS WITH SLIVERED ALMONDS

3 pounds fresh string beans
3 tablespoons butter
1 cup blanched white slivered almonds
1 teaspoon salt
¼ teaspoon freshly ground black pepper
2 teaspoons Maggi liquid seasoning (optional)

1. Trim the ends and pass the string beans through a French cutter or bean slicer, dividing them into two or three slices lengthwise.

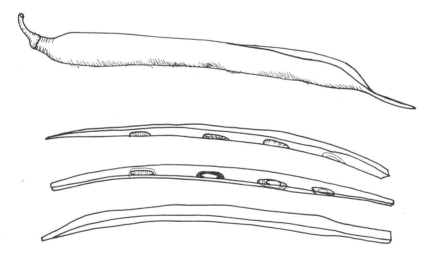

2. Steam the cut beans on a steamer platform over boiling water in a fairly deep, covered saucepan for 20 minutes.

3. While the beans are steaming, melt the butter in a skillet, add the slivered almonds, and stir them over medium heat until they brown slightly.

4. When the beans are done, remove them from the steamer, toss them in a bowl with the almonds and their butter, add the salt, pepper, and optional Maggi, and serve hot.

STEAMED ZUCCHINI WITH PARMESAN CHEESE

6 fresh zucchini, 5 to 6 inches long
¼ pound butter, softened
1½ cups grated Parmesan cheese

1. Wash the zucchini thoroughly. Arrange the zucchini on a steamer platform in a large covered saucepan over boiling water, cover, and steam for 15 minutes or until tender but not splitting.

2. Set the pan of the oven broiler at the maximum distance from heat and preheat broiler. Handling the zucchini with tongs, remove them from the steamer, lay them on a cutting board, and cut them in half lengthwise with a sharp knife. Arrange them in a shallow ovenproof dish, cut side up.

3. In a bowl, cream the softened butter together with the cheese.

4. Spread the cut sides of the zucchini with the cheese mixture. Place under the broiler and cook about 3 minutes until the surface of the cheese begins to brown slightly. Serve at once.

AVOCADO AND CARROT MOLD

1½ envelopes unflavored gelatin
1½ cups dry ginger ale
2 tablespoons fresh lemon juice, strained
1 cup grated raw carrots
2 large avocados, pitted and cut into balls

1. Dissolve the gelatin in the ginger ale over low heat in a saucepan until all the grains have disappeared. Add lemon juice and turn off heat.

2. Pour the liquid to a depth of ⅛ inch in a 5- to 6-cup ring mold; refrigerate until jelled.

3. Arrange clumps of grated carrots and avocado balls in an alternating pattern in the mold, fill with remaining liquid, and refrigerate until a few minutes before serving.

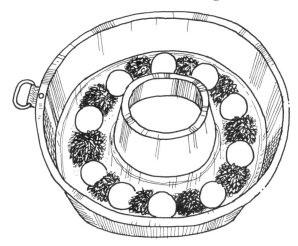

4. To serve, unmold by dipping the mold in hot water for a few seconds then reversing onto a serving platter.

CARROT AND RAISIN SALAD

8 to 10 large carrots
1 cup black raisins
1 teaspoon salt
¼ teaspoon freshly ground white pepper
2 teaspoons lemon juice
1½ cups sour cream

1. Peel the carrots and cut off tops. Grate them through the medium blade of a grater into a bowl, or use an electric food processor for grating.

2. Add the remaining ingredients, toss well to break up and distribute the sour cream, and let stand at least 1 hour before serving. Toss again just before serving.

CREAMED COLESLAW

1 medium-size head of green cabbage
1 medium to large onion
1 cup plain yogurt
½ cup mayonnaise
¼ cup white vinegar
2 teaspoons seasoned salt
1 teaspoon paprika
2 teaspoons caraway seeds

1. Remove any discolored leaves from the outside of the cabbage, wash the head, and shred it fine.

2. Peel and cut the onion into paper-thin slices. Toss in a bowl with the cabbage to mix well.

3. Mix yogurt, mayonnaise, vinegar, salt, paprika, and caraway seeds, pour this mixture over the cabbage and onion, and toss thoroughly.

4. Press slaw down in bowl to make sure all is moist, cover with plastic wrap, and refrigerate several hours before serving.

CUCUMBER SALAD WITH SOUR CREAM AND DILL

3 large fresh, firm cucumbers
¾ cup white vinegar
½ cup fresh chopped dill *or* ¼ cup dried dill weed
1½ cups sour cream
1 tablespoon lemon juice
½ teaspoon seasoned salt
¼ teaspoon freshly ground white pepper

1. Peel the cucumbers with a potato peeler, then slice them into very thin slices, about ⅛ inch thick.

2. Toss the slices in a bowl with the white vinegar and dill and let stand 1 hour.

3. Drain off the vinegar, add the sour cream, lemon juice, salt, and pepper, mix well, and serve. For decoration you may garnish with a sprig of fresh dill or parsley.

GREEN SALAD WITH LEMON DRESSING

This salad is very light and refreshing. It offers a nice contrast to a fairly heavy main course or goes particularly well with a summer luncheon. I advise making the dressing first, in the salad bowl you plan to bring to the table, then adding the greens and tossing. Salad should never be prepared in individual bowls with the dressing poured on afterward because this makes it impossible to coat the leaves with the dressing properly.

LEMON DRESSING

6 tablespoons olive oil (best-quality French, if possible)
3 tablespoons lemon juice
2 teaspoons sugar
½ teaspoon salt
¼ teaspoon freshly ground white pepper
1 tablespoon very finely minced fresh chives *or* frozen *or* dried minced chives
1 tablespoon very finely minced fresh parsley

1. Place the oil, lemon juice, and sugar in the salad bowl and mix well, dissolving the sugar.

2. Add all the remaining ingredients, mix, and let stand until just before time to serve the salad.

GREEN SALAD

1 large head bibb *or* Boston lettuce
1 bunch watercress
4 fresh scallions, sliced fine, including the green ends
1 cucumber, peeled and sliced thin

1. Tear apart the lettuce, wash each leaf under cold running water, tear into pieces about 1½ inches square, and lay them out on paper towels to drain and dry. This step is important, to assure that the dressing later coats the dry leaves thoroughly and to avoid diluting the dressing with water.

2. Wash and cut off the thick stems of the watercress. Dry the leaves in the same way as the lettuce.

3. Add the drained lettuce and watercress to the dressing in the salad bowl, followed by the chopped scallions and sliced cucumber.

4. Toss the salad thoroughly and serve.

SALADE RUSSE

(Mixed Vegetable Salad)

This salad is perfect for a buffet meal because it can easily be made quite decorative and provides a vegetable course where it might be difficult to serve vegetables hot.

½ pound fresh corn kernels, scraped off the cob
½ pound fresh peas, shelled
½ pound fresh string beans, cut into 1-inch pieces
2 medium-size potatoes
2 large carrots
1 cup peeled and diced cucumber
8 fresh white mushrooms, sliced
2 tablespoons chopped pimientos
2 tablespoons finely chopped green pepper
2 tablespoons finely minced sweet pickle
¼ pound cooked ham, sliced
4 anchovy fillets
2 to 3 cups mayonnaise
1 green olive

1. On a steamer platform over boiling water, steam, in turn, the corn kernels, peas, and string beans until just tender, about 8 minutes each for the corn and peas and 12 minutes for the beans. Place them in a large mixing bowl together after cooking.

2. Peel and boil the potatoes, and peel and boil the carrots until tender, about 15 to 20 minutes depending on size, in salted water to cover. When cool, dice them and add them to the bowl with the other vegetables.

3. Add the cucumbers, mushrooms, pimientos, green pepper, and pickle to the bowl.

4. Cut the ham slices into ½-inch squares and add them to the salad.

5. Mince the anchovy fillets and add them.

6. Add 2 cups of mayonnaise to the vegetables and toss well until everything is mixed and the salad is fairly sticky. The salad may be served as is or could be chilled as suggested below.

7. For decoration, reverse the bowl full of salad onto a serving platter, creating a fairly even, rounded mound. Using a wide

spreader or flexible bladed spatula, spread a thin layer of additional mayonnaise over the mound, producing an all-white hemisphere. Decorate with the green olive on top (or other vegetable arrangement such as crossed pimiento strips, or a slice of hardcooked egg) and chill until serving time.

TOMATO AND BERMUDA ONION SALAD

4 tablespoons olive oil
2 tablespoons red wine vinegar
½ teaspoon salt
¼ teaspoon freshly ground black pepper
1 large Bermuda onion
4 just-ripe tomatoes
2 tablespoons fresh chopped chives

1. In a shallow dish or soup plate combine the oil, vinegar, salt, and pepper.

2. Peel the onion and slice it into paper-thin slices. Lay the slices in the dressing so that they are covered with liquid. Marinate at least 1 hour, agitating dish occasionally to moisten the onion slices

3. To serve, slice the tomatoes, put them in a salad bowl, add the onions and dressing, toss, sprinkle chives over the top of salad, and serve.

CHEESE-STUFFED TOMATOES

6 medium-size just-ripe tomatoes
2 small dill pickles
1 apple
¼-pound piece Swiss cheese
¼ cup pitted black olives
½ cup mayonnaise
½ teaspoon salt
¼ teaspoon freshly ground black pepper

1. Slice off the tops of the tomatoes, scoop out pulp carefully without puncturing skin, drain the pulp on paper towels, and reserve the tops.

2. Dice the pickles; peel, core, and dice the apple; dice the cheese; cut up the olives. Combine all these with the tomato pulp in a bowl. Mix in the mayonnaise to blend well.

3. Salt and pepper the insides of the tomato shells, stuff with the mixture, piling higher than the cut, top with the tomato caps, and chill until serving time.

VIII

Desserts

BAKED APPLES WITH CURRANT JELLY

6 large apples
6 tablespoons brown sugar
2 tablespoons red currant jelly
2 tablespoons unsalted butter, softened
1 cup heavy cream, chilled

1. Preheat oven to 375 degrees.

2. Using an apple corer, remove cores from stem end down toward bottom of apples, but do not cut through all the way. To do this, compare length of corer with height of apple before starting to cut. Peel the upper one-third of the apples.

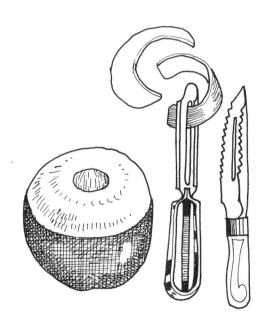

3. Arrange the apples in an ovenproof baking dish, place 1 tablespoon brown sugar and 1 teaspoon currant jelly in each apple cavity, then top with 1 teaspoon soft butter.

4. Pour enough boiling water into the baking dish to reach a depth of ⅛ inch. Bake in the preheated oven 40 minutes, basting occasionally. Serve either hot or cold with chilled cream.

CINNAMON APPLE PIE WITH CHEDDAR CHEESE

1 cup all-purpose flour
½ teaspoon salt
4 tablespoons butter, chilled
3 tablespoons vegetable shortening, chilled
2 tablespoons water
8 to 10 apples
1 cup sugar
1 teaspoon ground cinnamon
1 cup grated cheddar cheese

1. Sift the flour and salt together into a mixing bowl. Using two knives or a pastry blender, cut the butter and shortening into the flour until well combined.

2. Sprinkle on water and gather into a mass. Shape dough into a ball and blend it on a pastry board by spreading a little at a time with the heel of your hand. Gather into a ball again, dust lightly with flour, wrap in waxed paper, and refrigerate for at least 1 hour.

3. Preheat oven to 425 degrees.

4. Peel, quarter, core, and cut apples into bite-size chunks. Toss them in a bowl with the sugar and cinnamon.

5. Remove dough from refrigerator and roll out into a circle about 11 inches in diameter. Lay pastry in a 9-inch pie dish, fit in carefully, and crimp edges on lip of pie dish. Prick the pastry all over the bottom with a fork at 1-inch intervals.

6. Lay the apples in the pastry with the surface as level as possible. Bake in the preheated oven 50 minutes.

7. Sprinkle an even layer of the grated cheddar over the apples and return to the oven for another 5 minutes, or until cheese has just melted and browned slightly in one or two places. Serve hot.

BAKED BANANAS IN RUM

5 tablespoons unsalted butter
1 dozen bananas
4 tablespoons granulated sugar
4 tablespoons dark rum
½ teaspoon ground cinnamon

1. Preheat oven to 400 degrees. Using 1 tablespoon butter, grease a large ovenproof baking dish.

2. Peel and split the bananas lengthwise. Arrange them in one layer in the buttered baking dish.

3. In a small saucepan over low heat, melt the rest of the butter, add the sugar and rum, and stir while sugar dissolves completely.

4. Pour the rum mixture over the bananas, sprinkle the cinnamon over them, and bake in the preheated oven 20 minutes, basting occasionally.

5. To serve, bring the baking dish to the table, serve portions using a wide spatula, and spoon some liquid from the dish over each serving.

BREAD PUDDING SOUFFLÉ

6 eggs, separated
½ cup granulated sugar
1 tablespoon vanilla extract
1 cup white bread crumbs
1 teaspoon nutmeg
1 tablespoon butter, melted
1 tablespoon butter, softened
2 tablespoons bread crumbs, toasted
2 cups heavy cream, chilled
2 tablespoons powdered sugar

1. Preheat oven to 350 degrees.

2. In the bowl of an electric mixer, beat the egg yolks together with the granulated sugar until light-colored and creamy. Beat in vanilla extract.

3. Stir the white bread crumbs, nutmeg, and melted butter into the mixture.

4. In a separate bowl beat the egg whites until they form stiff peaks. Fold the whites gently into the first mixture.

5. Grease an 8-cup soufflé dish with the softened butter and coat the inner surfaces with the toasted bread crumbs.

6. Turn the pudding mixture into the prepared dish and bake in the preheated oven 30 minutes until puffed up and browned.

7. During baking, beat the heavy cream with the powdered sugar until soft peaks are formed. Chill the sweet whipped cream.

8. To serve, bring pudding to table and garnish each portion of hot pudding with a generous spoonful of the cream.

BROWNIES

¼ pound unsalted butter
5 1-ounce squares semisweet cooking chocolate
4 eggs
¼ teaspoon salt
2 cups granulated sugar
1 teaspoon almond extract
1 cup all-purpose flour
1 cup toasted almonds, broken up

1. Preheat oven to 350 degrees.

2. Melt the butter with the chocolate over very low heat in an enameled saucepan, stirring constantly and removing from heat as soon as chocolate has melted and mixture is smooth.

3. In a large mixing bowl beat the eggs with the salt until well blended and foamy. Continue beating, adding the sugar until all is absorbed. Finally, mix in the chocolate-butter mixture and the almond extract at slowest speed.

4. Sift the flour into the batter and fold it in with a rubber spatula until well distributed. Mix in the almonds in the same way.

5. Pour the batter into a 9-by-13-by-1-inch jelly-roll pan and bake in the preheated oven 30 minutes.

6. Remove from oven and allow brownies to cool to room temperature. Cut them into squares or rectangles in the pan, then remove with a spatula.

CHOCOLATE LAYER CAKE

¼ pound butter
1¾ cups granulated sugar
4 eggs, separated
2 cups cake flour
1 teaspoon double-acting baking powder
½ teaspoon baking soda
¼ teaspoon salt
10 tablespoons powdered cocoa
1¼ cups milk
1 teaspoon vanilla extract
1 pint heavy cream, chilled
2 tablespoons powdered confectioners' sugar

1. With an electric mixer cream the butter with the granulated sugar, adding sugar a little at a time until the mixture is light. Then continue beating, adding egg yolks one at a time.

2. Sift the flour with the baking powder, soda, salt, and 8 tablespoons of the cocoa. Beat about half the dry ingredients into the mixture, beat in the milk, then the rest of the dry ingredients, and finally the vanilla.

3. Preheat oven to 325 degrees.

4. In a separate bowl beat the egg whites until they form stiff peaks. Fold them gently into the batter.

5. Pour the batter, equally divided, into two 9-inch cake pans. Bake in the preheated oven for 1 hour until firm. Cake testing needle should come out clean.

6. When cake layers are done, reverse them onto cooling racks and let them cool while you prepare the filling.

7. Beat the heavy cream in the electric mixer until it forms soft peaks, then add the 2 remaining tablespoons cocoa and the powdered sugar. Continue beating just until color is even, no more. Chill until cakes cool to room temperature.

8. On a cake plate spread a layer of the chocolate cream over one layer of cake. Top with second cake layer, cover top and sides with cream, and refrigerate until serving time.

OPTIONAL: Decorate frosting with chocolate sprinkles, a glazed cherry, a pinch of grated coconut, a star of white almonds, or other garnish.

CHOCOLATE CHIP COOKIES
WITH WALNUTS

4 tablespoons unsalted butter
4 tablespoons vegetable shortening
¼ cup brown sugar
½ cup granulated sugar
1 egg
1 teaspoon vanilla extract
1 cup all-purpose flour
1 pinch salt
½ teaspoon baking soda
1 6-ounce package chocolate chips
¾ cup walnut meats, broken up

1. Preheat oven to 350 degrees.

2. Using an electric mixer combine the butter, shortening, and brown and white sugars until fluffy.

3. Beat the egg separately with the vanilla, then mix into the butter-sugar mixture.

4. Sift the flour with the salt and soda into the batter; mix in thoroughly.

5. Stir chocolate chips and walnuts into the batter, just enough to distribute evenly.

6. Grease a cookie sheet with butter; place 1 heaping teaspoonful of batter on the sheet for each cookie, keeping them about 2 inches apart. Bake 10 minutes until the cookies have spread out and browned.

7. Carefully remove the cookies from the sheet with a spatula onto a cooling rack, then bake the next batch. Continue until all are done. This recipe makes about 3 dozen cookies.

RICH CHOCOLATE MOUSSE

4 1-ounce squares semisweet cooking chocolate
1½ tablespoons strong coffee
1 teaspoon vanilla extract
5 eggs, separated
4 tablespoons granulated sugar
1 cup heavy cream, chilled
6 maraschino cherries

1. Over simmering water in a double boiler, melt the chocolate squares with the coffee, stirring until smooth. Off heat stir in the vanilla.

2. Using either a wire whisk or a hand-held electric mixer, beat the egg yolks, one at a time, into the chocolate mixture off heat.

3. Separately, beat the egg whites with an electric mixer, adding the sugar 1 tablespoon at a time until all is incorporated and the mixture is stiff. Combine egg-white mixture with the chocolate, folding to get an even color.

4. Beat the cream until it forms stiff peaks, then fold it gently into the chocolate mixture.

5. Spoon the mousse into tall stemmed glasses and chill several hours before serving. Top each portion with a cherry and bring to table.

CHOCOLATE ROLL WITH CREAM FILLING

6 eggs, separated
¾ cup confectioners' powdered sugar
2 teaspoons vanilla extract
½ cup powdered cocoa
2 tablespoons cake flour
1 teaspoon cream of tartar
1 cup heavy cream

1. Preheat oven to 325 degrees.

2. With an electric mixer beat together the egg yolks and ½ cup powdered sugar until smooth and creamy. Beat in the vanilla, ¼ cup of the cocoa, and the flour.

3. Separately, beat the egg whites with the cream of tartar until they form stiff peaks. Fold them gently into the first mixture.

4. Cut waxed paper to fit a standard jelly-roll pan and line the bottom with it. Pour in the batter and bake 30 minutes in the preheated oven. The waxed paper will prevent the thin "cake" from sticking.

5. Remove from oven and allow the chocolate roll to cool while preparing the cream.

6. Beat the cream with the remaining ¼ cup of powdered sugar until stiff.

7. Reverse the cake onto a slightly damp towel on a flat surface. Peel off the waxed paper. Spread the top with the cream filling evenly.

8. Roll up the cake like a jelly roll, using the towel to assist. Sprinkle the roll with the remaining ¼ cup of cocoa rubbed through a fine strainer.

9. Slip finished cake onto a serving platter or board. Keep refrigerated until serving time.

DESSERT CREPES

Here is a dependable last-minute dessert idea for those unexpected guests or when your family is still hungry after the main course and nothing much was planned for dessert. It requires only a few minutes of patience.

1 tablespoon butter, melted
1½ cups all-purpose flour
1 tablespoon granulated sugar
4 eggs
2 cups milk
¼ pound butter, softened, for frying crepes
   assorted jams and jellies
   powdered sugar

1. Combine the melted butter, flour, sugar, eggs, and milk in a mixing bowl and mix with egg beater or electric mixer until smooth.

2. Heat a crepe pan or small skillet over medium-high flame. Using about ½ tablespoon of butter for each crepe, melt the butter in the pan; pour in just enough batter to make a thin coating over the entire surface.

3. Shake pan to distribute batter evenly. Cook until edges begin to brown slightly, then flip crepe over, using a thin, flexible spatula. Cook a few seconds and reverse crepe onto a board.

4. As each crepe is finished, quickly spread one side with about 1 tablespoon of jam or jelly, roll up, sprinkle with powdered sugar, and either serve immediately or place on a platter until enough are done to take to the table.

FRUIT SALAD

There are few desserts as popular, refreshing, and satisfying as a really well-planned and executed fruit salad. The following fruit salads have no connection with the indifferent, overchilled, typical "fruit cup" we have all seen too often, characterized by wedges of apple, a slice or two of canned grapefruit and orange, topped by a maraschino cherry or sad, pale strawberry for "color." Use only fresh fruits, remove *all* inedible matter (including the bitter white inner skin from orange and grapefruit sections), provide a good variety of taste and texture, pay some attention to color, and you can't miss!

FRUIT SALAD I

2 apples
2 pears
2 peaches
4 purple plums
4 apricots
½ pound cherries
1 cup strawberries
1 medium-size cantaloupe
¼ watermelon
2 cups seedless green grapes
½ cup lemon juice
¼ cup kirsch
½ cup granulated sugar

1. Peel, quarter, core, and cut the apples and pears into bite-size pieces.

2. Peel, pit, and cut the peaches and plums into bite-size pieces.

3. Pit and cut the apricots into bite-size pieces. Cut the cherries in half and pit them.

4. Wash and hull the strawberries; cut any large ones into two or more pieces.

5. Ball the cantaloupe and the watermelon, making sure to remove all watermelon seeds. Wash and separate the seedless grapes from the vine.

6. Combine all the prepared fruit in a decorative bowl. Combine the lemon juice, kirsch, and sugar, stirring until sugar is dissolved, and pour the liquid over the fruit salad. Toss very gently with two large slotted spoons.

7. Refrigerate the fruit salad until about 1 hour before serving time. It should be allowed to return to room temperature. Serve in bowls, not on flat plates, to allow plenty of juice in each portion.

FRUIT SALAD II (TROPICAL)

1 large (or 2 small) mangoes
1 medium-size pineapple
3 navel oranges
3 bananas
8 ripe fresh figs
1 small Persian melon
6 guavas
1 small papaya
½ cup pineapple juice
½ cup grapefruit juice
½ cup granulated sugar

1. Peel the mangoes with a very sharp knife; cut the pieces of flesh away from the pit. Do not try to remove the pit by cutting the fruit in half because it is too firmly anchored to the flesh in the center.

2. Cut off top and bottom of the pineapple, then cut off rough exterior, making sure to remove all the needle-sharp thorns. Cut into slices, remove hard central core from each slice, then cut each slice into quarters or smaller pieces.

3. Remove all rind from the oranges, then cut into sections, removing all skin and seeds.

4. Peel and slice the bananas.

5. Peel the figs very carefully, and slice each one into three or four pieces.

6. Ball the Persian melon.

7. Pit and cut the guavas into bite-size pieces.

8. Ball the papaya, removing all the black seeds from the center.

9. Combine all the prepared fruit in a decorative bowl. Combine the pineapple juice, grapefruit juice, and sugar and mix until the sugar dissolves, then pour over fruit. Toss gently with two large slotted spoons.

10. Serve the fruit salad at room temperature or slightly chilled if weather is very hot.

ICE CREAM/SHERBET MOLD

This idea is simply to combine two or more flavors of ice cream and sherbet to create a multicolored frozen dessert. The principal ingredient is patience, and the assembly should be done well in advance of serving time, preferably the day before.

3 pints of ice cream and/or sherbet in two to six flavors

1. Let the first flavor of ice cream or sherbet, which will be at the top of the unmolded dessert, soften at room temperature until it is just liquid enough to pour.

2. Meanwhile, place a 6-cup-capacity (3-pint) decorative metal mold in the freezer.

3. If you desire a slanted effect in the dessert, arrange inside the freezer some object that will allow you to rest the mold at an angle without danger of falling over. Pour the softened ice cream into the mold and return it to the freezer. If you set it flat you will have a level layer. Take out the next flavor to soften.

4. When the first batch has hardened completely, pour in the second, replace in the freezer, slant if desired, take out the next flavor, and repeat the process until the mold is full. Remember that no matter what angles you use and what the shape of the final cavity is, the 6-cup mold will be filled completely by 3 pints of ice cream or sherbet.

5. Another method of mixing flavors in a frozen mold is to pour in the first flavor, let it begin to freeze, then insert one or more small glass jars or heavy glasses into it, creating holes. After freezing, the glasses may be removed and the cavities created filled with other flavors.

6. To serve, dip the mold in hot water for a few seconds, reverse onto a serving dish, and slice at the table.

LEMON PIE

CRUST INGREDIENTS

1 cup flour
½ teaspoon salt
1 tablespoon granulated sugar
6 tablespoons vegetable shortening
3 tablespoons cold water

FILLING INGREDIENTS

2 teaspoons grated lemon rind
¼ cup fresh lemon juice
2 tablespoons very soft butter
2 tablespoons cake flour
1 cup granulated sugar
2 eggs, separated
1 cup half and half (½ milk, ½ cream)

1. Sift the flour, salt, and sugar together into a bowl, cut the vegetable shortening into the dry ingredients, and rub with fingertips to combine. Add cold water, gather dough into a mass, and knead briefly to blend fat and flour. Roll into a ball, wrap in waxed paper, and refrigerate 1 hour.

2. Roll out the chilled dough into an 11-inch circle. Line a 9-inch pie plate with the dough, trimming edges and crimping a decorative pattern with a fork around the rim. Perforate bottom of dough with a fork at 1-inch intervals, then refrigerate the filled pie plate until filling is ready.

3. Preheat oven to 375 degrees.

4. In a mixing bowl beat together the lemon rind, juice, and soft butter to blend well. Beat in cake flour and sugar. Beat in egg yolks, one at a time, then the half and half.

5. Separately, beat the egg whites until they form stiff peaks. Stir one-third of the whites into the lemon mixture, then fold the rest of the whites into it gently.

6. Turn the lemon filling into the lined pie plate and place it in the preheated oven. Immediately reduce heat setting to 350 degrees, and bake 30 minutes until filling is golden brown and slightly puffed, and the edges of the crust have colored a little. Serve hot or cold.

HOT PECAN PIE

CRUST INGREDIENTS

1 cup flour
½ teaspoon salt
6 tablespoons vegetable shortening
3 tablespoons cold water

FILLING INGREDIENTS

3 eggs
¼ teaspoon salt
2 teaspoons vinegar
2 teaspoons vanilla extract
¾ cup brown sugar
¾ cup corn syrup
1 cup pecan halves

1. For the crust, sift the flour with the salt into a mixing bowl, then cut the shortening into the dry ingredients. Blend with two knives or a pastry blender until the mixture has the appearance of corn meal. Add cold water, gather into a mass, knead well, roll into a ball, and refrigerate for about 15 minutes, wrapped in waxed paper.

2. Roll out the dough to a 10- to 11-inch circle and line a 9-inch pie plate, crimping dough around the edges. Perforate bottom of dough at 1-inch intervals with a fork.

3. Preheat oven to 400 degrees.

4. Beat the eggs and salt together with an electric mixer, then beat in vinegar, vanilla, sugar, and syrup only until well blended.

5. Line the pie dough with a thick layer of pecan halves, pour the liquid over them, and bake in preheated oven for 30 minutes or until the surface of the pie is set and the crust is golden brown around the edges.

6. Serve the pie hot if possible. If not, serve at room temperature, but do not refrigerate.

PINEAPPLE UPSIDE-DOWN CAKE

¼ pound unsalted butter
2 cups brown sugar
6 to 8 slices canned *or* fresh pineapple
6 to 8 maraschino cherries
4 eggs, separated
1 cup granulated sugar
1 cup all-purpose flour
1 teaspoon double-acting baking powder
1 pinch salt

1. Preheat oven to 350 degrees.

2. Melt the butter, combine with the brown sugar, then spread an even layer of this mixture in the bottom of a heavy cast-iron or enameled ovenproof 9- to 10-inch skillet at least 2 inches deep.

3. Arrange the pineapple slices on surface of the butter/sugar mixture and place a cherry in the center of each slice.

4. Using an electric mixer, beat the egg yolks and granulated sugar together until light-colored and smooth. Sift the flour and baking powder together into the yolk mixture and fold in thoroughly.

5. Separately, beat the egg whites with the salt until they form stiff peaks. Fold the whites into the yolk-flour mixture, just enough to distribute evenly. Pour this batter over the pineapple slices in the skillet.

6. Bake in the preheated oven for 40 minutes. Remove from oven, allow to cool for 10 or 15 minutes. Pass a sharp knife around the edges of the cake, then reverse onto a serving platter. The cake may be served warm, at room temperature, or chilled.

PLAIN POUND CAKE

A wonderful, satisfying cake to have on hand, pound cake can be used for breakfast toast, as an accompaniment for fresh fruit salad, along with ice cream, and in many other ways.

½ pound butter, softened
1 cup granulated sugar
6 eggs, separated
1 teaspoon vanilla extract
2 cups cake flour, sifted
¼ teaspoon salt

1. Preheat oven to 350 degrees.

2. Using an electric mixer, beat all but 1 tablespoon of the softened butter with the sugar until well blended.

3. Beat in the egg yolks, one at a time, and then vanilla extract. Add the sifted cake flour, a little at a time, beating it in at slow speed until all is incorporated.

4. Separately, beat the egg whites with the salt until they form stiff peaks. Stir one-third of the beaten whites into the other mixture, then gently fold the remaining whites in.

5. Butter a 9-by-4-by-4-inch loaf pan with the remaining 1 tablespoon softened butter.

6. Turn the batter into the pan and bake in the preheated oven 1 hour, until the top of the cake is browned and the sides have pulled away from the pan.

7. Turn pound cake onto cooking rack and allow it to reach room temperature before slicing. To keep, wrap tightly in plastic wrap and refrigerate.

RASPBERRY AND ALMOND SOUFFLÉ

2 tablespoons unsalted butter, softened
2 tablespoons granulated sugar
3 10-ounce packages frozen raspberries in syrup, thawed
½ cup blanched almonds
½ teaspoon almond extract
6 egg whites
⅛ teaspoon salt

1. Preheat oven to 375 degrees.

2. Butter a 6-cup soufflé dish generously and dust with the sugar so that it adheres to the butter on all inner surfaces. Refrigerate the soufflé dish until ready to fill.

3. Rub the thawed raspberries with their liquid through a fine strainer to remove the seeds. Place strained berries in a heavy enameled saucepan and cook over medium heat, stirring occasionally, uncovered, for about 30 minutes.

4. Grind the almonds in a nut grinder or electric blender.

5. Combine the ground almonds, cooked raspberries, and almond extract in a large bowl. Separately, beat the egg whites with the salt until they form stiff peaks. Fold the whites into the raspberry mixture as gently as possible while achieving an even color throughout.

6. Pour the mixture into the prepared soufflé dish and bake in the middle level of the preheated oven for 20 minutes, until the soufflé has puffed up well above the edges of the dish and browned. Serve immediately.

RICE PUDDING AND RAISINS

2 cups cooked white rice
1¼ cups milk
½ cup brown sugar
2 teaspoons vanilla extract
2 tablespoons butter, melted
3 eggs, beaten
½ cup white raisins (which are much plumper than black raisins)
1 tablespoon butter, softened
2 tablespoons graham crackers
1 pint light cream, chilled

1. Preheat oven to 325 degrees.

2. In a mixing bowl combine the cooked rice, milk, brown sugar, vanilla, melted butter, beaten eggs, and raisins, stirring well to distribute ingredients evenly.

3. Butter an 8-inch baking dish with the softened butter and dust inner surfaces with graham-cracker crumbs.

4. Turn pudding mixture into the baking dish and bake in the preheated oven for 1 hour. Serve hot with chilled cream on the side.

STRAWBERRY SHORTCAKE

3 tablespoons vegetable shortening, softened
4 cups fresh strawberries
4 tablespoons granulated sugar
1 tablespoon kirsch
2 cups all-purpose flour
2 teaspoons double-acting baking powder
¼ teaspoon salt
6 tablespoons confectioners' powdered sugar
2 tablespoons unsalted butter, softened
½ cup milk
¼ cup water
1 cup heavy cream, chilled

1. Preheat oven to 425 degrees.

2. With 1 tablespoon shortening grease a cookie sheet and set aside.

3. Wash and hull the strawberries, halve them, toss them in a bowl with the granulated sugar and kirsch, and let stand while you are making the biscuits.

4. Sift together the flour, baking powder, salt, and 2 table-spoons of the powdered sugar. Using a pastry blender, blend in the softened butter and remaining shortening. With your hands, work the dough, adding the milk, then the water, until a smooth, malleable dough is formed which will hold its shape but is not too wet.

5. On a lightly floured pastry board roll the dough out to a thickness of about ½ inch. Cut into 4-inch circles with a cookie cutter, then place on greased cookie sheet. Bake in the pre-heated oven for 15 minutes or until golden brown. Remove from oven and allow the biscuits to cool to room temperature.

6. Beat the chilled cream with the remaining 4 tablespoons powdered sugar until it forms soft peaks.

7. To assemble dessert, split the biscuits with a fork. On each lower half spoon a generous portion of strawberries and some whipped cream. Add the top half of the biscuit, more strawberries, and top with one more spoonful of whipped cream.

INDEX